P9-AOS-672

Evolution or Revolution?

Evolution or Revolution?

The United Nations and the Problem of Peaceful Territorial Change

LINCOLN P. BLOOMFIELD

Harvard University Press
Cambridge, Massachusetts
1957

Distributed in Great Britain by Oxford University Press, London

Printed in the United States of America

Library of Congress Catalog Card Number 57–9070

to Iri

Acknowledgments

The author is especially indebted to the following for their guidance, assistance, or encouragement, absolving them at the same time of any responsibility for the results: Daniel S. Cheever, Inis L. Claude, Rupert Emerson, Robert W. Hartley, Virginia F. Hartley, Leonard C. Meeker, Dean Rusk, Eric Stein, Kenneth N. Thompson, and Roscoe E. Trueblood.

A fellowship from the Rockefeller Foundation made it possible to take time off from government service to write this book.

That a family of bureaucrats was able to make a temporary transition to academic life not only painlessly but gaily, was largely due to the person who, among untold other good offices, helped to edit and type the manuscript, and to whom this book is affectionately dedicated.

The views that follow are the author's own, and not necessarily those of the United States Government.

L.P.B.

Contents

Evolution or Revolution?

"De status quo? Dat's de mess we's already in"

Anonymous

All man's troubles come from his inability to sit still

Pascal

Introduction

The essence of history is change. —

Jacob Burckhardt, *Force and Freedom*

This book is about the process of change in the international status of territories, and how such changes may be brought about by means other than war. It is largely concerned with the role of the United Nations in this process. Its point of view is that of United States foreign policy.

As this work goes to press, new and dramatic examples are being furnished, in the Near East and Eastern Europe, of the powerful forces in the world that make for change, violent or peaceful. The dramas that have unfolded there had their roots in the past. They will play a part in shaping the future. And they serve to illustrate further the propositions that follow about the role of the United Nations in the process of peaceful change.

The risks inherent in thermonuclear warfare remain fundamentally intolerable to all nations, so long as reason is not driven out by desperation. Our era has been styled the age of limited wars, with accuracy, even with enlightened purpose, for the lesser evil is always to be preferred. And yet each new attempt to alter the established order by violence only proves once again that violent change tends to set up potentially uncontrollable circumstances in which justice can quickly lose its meaning.

Thus it is that in our time the words "peaceful change," rarely spoken since the 1930's, are being heard again. With each passing year of the nuclear age, these words ring with a more clamant urgency. If what is said in the pages ahead can help to endow this phrase with greater meaning and content, it will have served its purpose, whatever kind of world the reader finds about him when he comes to share in this quest.

The words "peaceful change" are imprecise, and convey a variety of different meanings. Only one of these meanings — the traditional one — is examined in this book.

"Peaceful change" can, of course, be taken to signify almost any transition in a country or group of countries from one condition to another, if the transition is accomplished without violence. It does not have to involve sovereignty or boundaries. "Peaceful change" could mean the type of profound internal change in policy that fundamentally alters a nation's course — the sort of change we ardently desire to witness within the Soviet Union, for instance.

A good case might also be made that the most significant "peaceful changes," particularly through international organizations, involve, not territorial status, but changes from a pastoral to an industrial economy through economic development programs, changes from the stone age to the twentieth century through introduction of the steel-tipped plow, and so on.

All of these may be peaceful change, and their importance is undeniable. Indeed, the United Nations' economic and social programs, no less than the political issues, have in common the coloration each receives from the dynamic nature of the United Nations as an institution. For as a political and social institution the United Nations, as its critics so well understand, tends to identify with the forces that make for change, rather than those that favor the *status quo*. In this respect it differs significantly from the League of Nations. Its inherent bias toward change powers much of the economic and social development mentioned above. The bias toward change also vitally affects the relation of the United Nations to the territorial problems that plague the nations, and in particular the "colonial problem." It is from the latter — the field of territorial issues — that this book takes its theme.

Territorial issues are often dismissed as anachronisms, particularly by those who find the most satisfying meaning for international organization in the so-called humanitarian programs. Curiously enough, however, frontiers are more jealously guarded in this age of enlightened international theories than they ever were in the days of outspoken imperialism. In the world of tomorrow boundaries and national sovereignty may perhaps become meaningless. But today they still have the capacity to constitute a *casus belli* for which a dozen, a thousand, or a hundred million lives may be sacrificed. The problem of change in the international status of territories is still a formidable one. It appears in the foreground of mankind's bloodiest wars, as well as its sharpest and most persistent international tensions.

So, until territorial issues really do become an anachronism, we would do well not to lose sight of the continuing and insistent presence, despite our dreams, our words, and our timid progress, of the age-old problems of whose territory, who wants it, how can he get it, who gets hurt, and where is the law?

This book, then, is about "peaceful change" in the sense of the transition of territories from one international political and legal status to another, primarily by nonviolent means. It is about the United Nations and the territorial problem as a concrete fact, rather than peaceful change as an abstract concept. It seeks for the meaning of the United Nations in the rhythms of history in which, in such traditional terms as boundaries and territorial sovereignty, the real estate of the world has been disputed by man since his memory runneth not to the contrary.

The dynamics of this process constitute "change" in a sense every citizen can often see, feel, and hear. If such change takes place primarily by nonviolent means, we can call it "peaceful change." This process has been at the center of international politics for centuries. In a very real sense, it still is.

Let us become specific. What are some of the contemporary tensions arising from the desire of one state for change in the international political or legal status of a territory possessed by another? The world of the mid-twentieth century is full of examples.

In Europe, West Germany wants East Germany and vice versa. Both Germanies presumably want East Prussia and the Polish-occupied lands east of the Oder-Neisse line. Ireland perennially agitates for the six counties of Northern Ireland. Austria is unhappy with Italian possession of the South Tyrol. Spain claims Gibraltar from Britain. The Soviet Union periodically demands a new regime in the Turkish Straits. Greece wants union with Cyprus. And the United States will probably not rest until there comes to pass a fundamental alteration in the dependent political status of East Germany, Poland, Czechoslovakia, Hungary, Rumania, Bulgaria, and Albania.

In Africa, both the indigenous inhabitants and the Arab states insist on the rapid and total independence from France of Algeria. The Union of South Africa wishes to annex SouthWest Africa, while a majority of the United Nations General Assembly regularly insists that it be placed under trusteeship. Ethiopia wants federation with Somaliland.

In the Middle East, Arab policy aims at extinguishing Israel's independent status, and in any event both Israel and its neighbors claim jurisdiction over borderlands in the areas left undefined in the armistice agreements. The Western nations consider that the Suez Canal has a character that is other than exclusively Egyptian. Saudi Arabia objects to Great Britain's position in the Buraimi oases. Both India and Pakistan want Kashmir. India wishes Portugal out of Goa. Afghanistan wants a new regime — "Pushtunistan" — for the

Northwest province area of Pakistan inhabited by Pathan tribesmen. Yemen wants Britain's Aden Protectorate.

In South East Asia, Indonesia persistently asserts claims to West New Guinea. North Vietnam wants to take over South Vietnam, just as the local communists would like to take over Cambodia and Laos. South Vietnam considers North Vietnam *irredentist* territory. Vietnam and China both claim the Paracel Islands and Spratly. Burma and Communist China dispute portions of their extensive border regions. Unassimilated portions of Indonesia have in the recent past voiced a desire for independence from Indonesia itself.

In the Far East, Japan wants back from the Soviet Union South Sakhalin, and Etorofu and Kunashiri of the Kurile Islands. From the United States, Japan wants back the Bonin and Ryukyu islands. Communist China wants Formosa and the offshore islands, and doubtless Hong Kong. The Chinese government on Formosa wants mainland China. South Korea wants North Korea and vice versa.

In Latin America, apart from the perpetually unsettled national borders, Argentina claims the Falkland Island Dependency from the United Kingdom, and its neighbors lay claim to British Honduras (Belize).

And even in the frozen wastes of the Antarctic, the last *terra nullius* in the world, a competition is steadily developing for territorial possessions.

The United Nations has become significantly involved in at least eleven of these issues. Others hover in the wings. Some of them could be resolved outside the organization. Some may not be resolved in our lifetime. Some could lead to war. All are involved in the question of peaceful change as we have defined it here.

Peaceful change is a process. It takes place over a period of time, short or long. It may occur by default, with no one doing anything about it, as so often happens when an international issue "solves" itself. Or it may be manipulated from start to finish by procedures including pacific settlements, bilateral or multilateral diplomatic negotiations, economic, social, and cultural policies, propaganda techniques, demonstrations of national or multinational power, threats of force, moral exhortations, and even, in rare instances, impartial arbitration or adjudication.

It is brought about by means that are primarily nonmilitary, in order that it may be called peaceful. Yet it is reduced to an abstract nullity if one excludes the presence of what C. B. Marshall called "the factor of force in the image which nations cast on the consciousness of other nations."[1] Peaceful change in the twentieth century is not invariably bloodless, and in any event it takes place in a setting of meaningful political forces.

In order to put this problem in perspective, this book, after a chapter setting forth the broad dimensions of the problem, examines the record respecting peaceful change of both the League of Nations and the United Nations (including some hitherto unpublished materials on the drafting of the "peaceful change" article of the United Nations Charter).

After a brief survey of the legal aspects of peaceful change as they appear to a non-lawyer, it concludes with a statement of the significance of peaceful change in the United Nations, as it affects United States foreign policy.

There is a bias in this work that should be made explicit. Its orientation is toward the world of policy rather than theory. In any contest of ideas within these covers between the theoretically good and the practically possible, the latter will usually win out. This is an inescapable byproduct of the writer's training and background as a public servant, since over those sixteen years the public interest seemed usually to be served by practical notions resting on sound general principles, and disserved by unattainable theoretical formulations.

This pragmatic and utilitarian bias, which seems to say,

with Bentham, "that which is politically good cannot be morally bad," sometimes invites charges ranging from short-sightedness to cynicism and even downright immorality. In its defense two pleas can be entered.

The first rests on such virtue as policy may have when it is at the same time right, correct, and successful.

The second distinguishes between the short-term and the long-term. No apology is needed for the attempt to harmonize theory with fact in order to produce a responsible and, if possible, successful public policy. But this does not mean that the accommodation must be made permanent, or that we should be blinded to the potentialities of men and societies for change, development, and maturation. Indeed, to rest on the intellectual and moral *status quo* would be not only stultifying in itself, but a travesty on the thesis presented in the following pages. For this work is dedicated to the proposition that change is inevitable, history is dynamic, and the *status quo* is an impermanent edifice that must constantly be revalued, revalidated, and reconstituted.

To follow these parallel paths, one walks not boldly but cautiously, even hesitantly. A theory, for example, that there "must" be a world legal order and that men should consequently behave as though it fully existed, will be found intellectually unacceptable, morally futile, and politically dangerous. This is a present judgment for which impressive evidence can be amassed. But it is a tentative judgment, subject, like all else, to alteration. The truly immoral act would be to foreclose the future by substituting fallible human prophecy for the "Spirit of the Earth, as he weaves and draws his threads on the Loom of Time." For, in the words of Arnold Toynbee:

> . . . though strophe may be answered by antistrophe, victory by defeat, creation by destruction, birth by death, the movement that this rhythm beats out is neither the fluctuation of an indecisive battle nor the cycle of a treadmill. The perpetual turning of a wheel is not a vain repetition if, at each revolution, it is carrying the vehicle that much nearer to its goal.[2]

Chapter 1

The Ideology of Peaceful Change

It is provided in the essence of things that from any fruition of success, no matter what, shall come forth something to make a greater struggle necessary. —
Walt Whitman

Few men in history have been willing to go on record in favor of freezing the *status quo* for all time. Invariably there has been the claim to be searching for a system in which stability could be preserved, yet changes assimilated. But more often than not change has been viewed as "lawful" only if made according to ground rules laid down under the authority of the dominant political and intellectual regime. That this applied to all shades of political opinion has been confirmed by the reactionary behavior of the revolutionaries in Moscow whenever they confront a question of the permanence of the regime. Indeed, Karl Marx once spoke of this in a way which it is doubtful his Russian disciples would appreciate:

> Each new class which puts itself in the place of one ruling before it, is compelled, merely in order to carry through its aim, to represent its interest as the common interest of all members of society . . . It will give its ideas the form of universality, and represent them as the only rational, universally valid ones.[1]

Few voices in the past, outside of such spokesmen for the French Reaction as De Maîstre and De Bonald, were heard to argue that change is always evil, or can in the long run be averted. Lawgivers and lawyers, whatever side they took, generally agreed with Aristotle, when he cautioned, "Nor is it . . . right to permit written laws always to remain without alteration." [2]

In 1576 Jean Bodin wrote that there always existed a strong tendency to revolution to combat inequalities, and that change was thus always inevitable.[3] Conservative thinkers have often appeared more aware of this than, for example, some nineteenth-century French liberals who "failed to see that the upholding of a law as something unalterable, even by legal methods, led straight to revolution." [4] Edmund Burke wrote that a state without means of change is without means of its own conservation,[5] and even Herbert Spencer echoed, "change is inevitable." [6]

But, even after having confessed that change is inevitable, political action seldom operated on Nietzsche's dictum that change is beyond good and evil. To recognize the inevitability of change did not have to mean evading its moral and ethical components. Only the historian of civilizations could lift his eyes from the contemporary scene and allow the procession of millenniums to tell their own grandiose story. Yet even Toynbee, in his sweeping panoramas and detached observation of the rhythms of history, struck a persistent note of voluntarism, of contingency, and of human design, denying with his same evidence that history is a mad horse plunging heedlessly through time and space.

As a guide to policy and action, it is not enough to fix as a basic and unalterable principle of human affairs that change is inevitable and that tensions always antecede, accompany, and follow change. A different tool than the telescope is needed to grapple with the modern situation, even to understand it. If, within the microcosm of one civilization in one epoch, the directives of history can be rewritten to a meaningful extent by man, the microscope is needed to reveal the details and disclose the possibilities for action that a long lens misses. The distant vision might deny these possibilities as inconsistent with the grand pattern. But the pattern is always in process of being fabricated, and history has not yet run its course.

IDEALISM, REALISM, AND INTERNATIONALISM

The building of human societies has called for common understandings and flexible political techniques in order that the inevitable tensions between stability and change could be moderated and lived with. Ways have been found to institutionalize stability and change in local communities and in states, within walls whose bricks were the laws but whose mortar was the social stuff of consent and legitimacy.

So, when men turned to the relations between states, it was natural to project into the anarchy of interstate politics the theories and techniques of social construction that had succeeded in building the world's communities. The paramount fact from which everyone had to start was that revolution could normally be avoided or suppressed at home, yet international revolution — war — so far had defied the norms of civilized life. International rule-making foundered on one terrible fact: there always seemed to be a new crop of men and societies who, like the ancient Athenians, "were born into the world to take no rest themselves and to give none to others." [7]

Yet the great mass of men and societies were not only willing but eager to live quietly and at peace. By the eighteenth century this yearning acquired the status of a political philosophy. Count Antoine Nicolas de Condorcet, a French nobleman turned liberal historian, stated the thesis for the generations that followed:

> . . . nature has set no term to the perfection of human faculties . . . the perfectibility of man is truly indefinite . . . Once . . . a close accord has been established between all enlightened men,

from then onwards all will be the friends of humanity, all will work together for its perfection and its happiness . . . The principles of philosophy, the slogans of liberty, the recognition of the true rights of man and his real interests, have spread through far too great a number of nations, and now direct in each of them the opinions of far too great a number of enlightened men, for us to fear that they will ever be allowed to relapse into oblivion.[8]

But soon new and dismaying evidence piled up that while man might be perfectible, his interstate arrangements continued to mock his rational, pacific and self-denying nature. Efforts were redoubled to transform international politics into the image of law and order and community. Doubts were stifled by repeating in different ways Disraeli's aphorism that "a realist is a man who insists on making the same mistakes his grandfather did." The derision of the skeptic was met with paraphrases of Lamartine's "Utopias are often only premature truths."

The twentieth century brought new and greater wars, and new and greater lawlessness. On rational grounds, the two world organizations of this age — the League of Nations and the United Nations — appeared to respond to an obvious objective need. But the new philosophy gave them the needful ideological sanction. For, without Kant's categorical imperative, without the revival of natural law, and, above all, without the modern belief in the essential rationality of man and the inevitability of progress, there would perhaps have been a new Concert of powers to meet the need, but hardly a universal organization speaking the language of law and postulating a will and interest on the part of states to take or desist from action in the name of transcendent norms.

Three strong currents ran counter to this tide of idealism. One was the growing awareness of defects in the doctrine of peace and progress as a natural corollary of the rational nature of man. Charles Darwin and Sigmund Freud contributed to this awareness, but in fact it stretched back through puritanical Calvinism to the dim recesses of the racial myth, where an apple and a serpent were the symbols of man's primordial fall from grace. "Caesars and saints," Reinhold Niebuhr reminded men, "are made possible by the same structure of human nature." [9] A secular theologian of politics echoed this theme:

> It is only the awareness of the tragic presence of evil in all political action which at least enables man to choose the lesser evil and to be as good as he can be in an evil world.[10]

Out of this pessimistic, "realistic" view, drawing heavily on the political prophecies of Machiavelli and Hobbes, a new school of thought emerged in this century, concentrating its fire on the fallacies of international political liberalism, and, above all, on the institutionalization of those fallacies in the League of Nations and the United Nations. It was as if the Enlightenment had been the modern Garden of Eden; the doctrine of human perfectibility, the great heresy; and, in this age, the eating of the apple of atomic knowledge the ultimate sin, for which man is to be punished.

The second countercurrent was the increasing realization that, despite the new norms, the world of nation-states was continuing to behave on the basis of particular rather than common interests. Coupled with this was the mounting evidence that "rebels" against the *status quo* could not often be dealt with effectively within a voluntary order characterized by plural power centers. If the Old Testament was proving an excessively gloomy Baedeker through the labyrinths of human nature, the story of creation, redemption, and resurrection was also failing as a model for "the idea that history is not a meaningless series of recurring cycles, but a drama with a unique and happy ending." [11]

And the third countercurrent made it even more difficult to maintain confidence in what an English anthropologist has called "this system of achieving morality by treating as nonexistent facts which cannot be reconciled with an ethical picture."[12] For the League of Nations existed as much to preserve with maximum rigidity the post-Versailles order, primarily for the benefit of France, as it did to provide a framework and set of techniques to maintain the peace. As an agency for inflexible support of the *status quo*, it was defying the whole political tradition that accepted inevitable change, even within the rubric of law and moral conduct.

The United Nations grew out of much the same philosophical and traditional setting as the League, but with two significant differences. First, the *status quo* was no longer something fixed in one set of dimensions, but was instead a multiple array of established orders, against each of which large-scale forces were in revolt. One *status quo* was the established social and economic order in the West, confronted by world communism armed with a military power and an international organization of its own never equalled in modern times. Second was the territorial *status quo* of the newly enriched communist empire in Europe and Asia, profoundly anathema to the Western democracies. And third was the colonial *status quo* in Africa, Asia, and the Middle and Near East, already in the process of being overthrown by the newly energized peoples of the colored races. The concepts of *status quo*, of revolution, and of progress, had all metamorphosed into new shapes; the United Nations, instead of being wedded to the *status quo*, had a distinct bias in favor of "change" and of "progress."

The second difference arose from the new quality of warfare.

THE OUTLAWRY OF WAR

All of the components of the notion of peaceful change came to a head at one cardinal point: the problem of war. For it was the recurrence of war, rather than any utopian dream of personal grace, that animated and continues to animate responsible liberal thinkers. The evils of the state system and the proven inability of men to practice successfully their civilized community practices on the world stage have had their ultimate, apocalyptic expression in the total wars of the twentieth century.

In the face of this recurring challenge to rationality and perhaps to survival, the "idealists" have always explained most reassuringly the nature of man and the ethos of international life. But the "realists" have seemed to describe the modern situation with greater accuracy. The one was a normative, ethical approach, valid within its own limits; the other was descriptive — a mirror image of the actual position. It was only when one pretended to be the other that moral and intellectual confusion growing out of extravagent claims began to substitute for rational debate. For, while both systems belong within the same universe of discourse, neither is identical with the other.

Outlawry of war was and is the ultimate goal of international morality and international organization. Those who sought this goal could concede that states in fact do operate on the basis of their particular interests. But this was because it fitted their conviction that the gap between particular and general interests had long since been bridged by the discovery that war was offensive to the rational nature of man; that there existed a natural harmony of interests achievable by pooling special interests; and that if only men would behave on the basis of rational premises, they would see that war was in no one's interest, whereas peace was in every man's.

This philosophy could make no headway so long as a strong nation was able to satisfy its desires cheaply and decisively through war. It commenced to make better sense as warfare became increasingly expensive, as goals were no longer readily satisfiable without taking account of the growing concern of other nations for international justice, and as the risks of failure came to involve grave damage to a nation's human as well as material resources.

By the second decade of this century there was almost universal popular revulsion against von Treitschke's dictum that war "must be taken as part of the divinely appointed order." The Kellogg-Briand Pact for the Renunciation of War, signed in Paris in 1928, was the expression of this widespread reformatory mood.

This Pact was condemned by some, not for having outlawed war, as it was believed for a time to have done, but, having outlawed war, for failing to provide a substitute for war. "Now that war has been abolished," the argument ran, "there must be an equivalent procedure for satisfying the pressures that build up to war." The conclusion was unassailable, but the premise was faulty. War had not been outlawed in any real sense, and it had not been abolished in any sense.

A group of jurists who mistook illusion for reality were genuinely concerned with the "gap" left by the Pact. It was consequently deplored in some circles for having destroyed the rude symmetry that had previously existed in international law. Prior to the Pact, international law had "made no provision for institutional peaceful change" but at the same time "permitted war as an instrument for changing the existing legal position." Now war was outlawed but no substitute instrument of change had been supplied.[13]

In the absence of meaningful political force behind the "law" abolishing war, the available moral equivalents were totally insufficient, and the problem of providing a legal substitute for war was, in this sense, a fantasy. Force had been legally banned but some powerful states, even after consulting their rational interests, still agreed with Clausewitz that war was a continuation of policy by other means. If they had to have war to satisfy national ambitions or needs, it would be enough of a genuflection to the new legal spirit to claim legality on their side, and to dress up policy in the language of the ideology of peace and law.

Yet, as of today, while "small wars" that could become big ones dominate our morning papers year in and year out, a major, total, nuclear war, on the evidence that is accumulating, still seems unlikely rather than likely. The objective facts about modern weapons systems and their potentialities for indiscriminate destruction have, for the first time in history, brought the major powers, possibly including the Soviet Union, to what Bernard Brodie has called "the end of strategy." [14]

On the basis of this profound fact it is tempting to reach two conclusions. Now, for the first time, general war will not in fact take place, since in reality as well as in theory it is contrary to the interests of nations. Since change is inevitable, peaceful change will automatically take the place of violent change.

But these conclusions are misleading to the point of being dangerous, without importantly qualifying them. Regarding the first, the quantum jump in the technology of warfare is still contingent on the same variables that disabled earlier advances in the technology of peace. The formulation of rules of international law, the signing of treaties, even the demonstrable values of pacific settlements of disputes, have always been subject to the irrational behavior of men and states, and to a totally different evaluation of rational interests on both sides of the *status quo*. So the discovery that nuclear warfare might be suicidal for both sides depends for its validity not alone on the "peace-loving state," whose intuition it merely confirms, but on its equal acceptability to the rebellious state which in other times would have gambled on war for what it could concretely achieve.

Regarding the second conclusion, peaceful change, when the established order is under major attack, has always been a possibility if the ambitions or grievances of the challenger were limited, concrete, politically finite, and therefore satisfiable with concessions based on principles of justice, equity, law, or just plain common sense. But already in this century the world has been exposed to ambitions that seemed limitless and international revolution that was nihilistic.

One authority, calling such total drives "imperialistic," was careful to exclude from this category the situations

> . . . when a state, no matter how brutally and vigorously, pursues concrete interests of its own; and when it can be expected to abandon its aggressive attitude as soon as it has attained what it was after.

Imperialism, he continued, implies "aggressiveness, the true reasons for which do not lie in the aims which are temporarily being pursued." It is rather "the objectless disposition on the part of a state to unlimited forcible expansion." [15]

Today, as before, it can be safely assumed that such situations as the aspirations of India for Goa, of Afghanistan for "Pushtunistan," of Indonesia for West New Guinea, of Spain for Gibraltar, and of the Arab states for a change in the status of French North Africa, are all susceptible to ultimate peaceful accommodation, particularly if there is a contingent threat of force or of involvement in an unmanageable and unwanted war. But procedures of peaceful change at their very best might not have changed the course of the Napoleonic Wars, or of Hitler's drive for world mastery. The ambitions of democratic nations are generally finite ambitions, concretely satisfiable. But what of world communism?

All the evidence suggests that the communist conviction of universal revolution constitutes a total grievance, not susceptible to satisfaction within the existing legal and political order. Yet communists, on their own terms, are rational men too. They can conclude that war is not a feasible means of achieving their ends, and, indeed, their policies have faltered, as in Finland and Korea, only when they have ignored this truth. This does not mean that communism's demands on world society can or should always be met and accommodated by peaceful means. It does not mean that, because the communists are not prepared to fight the West, it automatically follows that they are prepared to negotiate. Nor does it mean that communism has permanently renounced the use of force to gain its ultimate ends, if the price should ever again appear to be a reasonable one.

It should never be forgotten that nuclear warfare is not the only kind available. Savage wars can still be fought with conventional arms, and estimates of the Soviet Union's view of war as an instrument of policy must take into account that regime's recurrent insistence that nuclear arms be outlawed, but conventional arms merely reduced.

Still, to say that general war fought with nuclear weapons is a mutually shared nightmare is to have said a good deal, and among other things it made this book seem worth writing. But it still leaves the detailed problem of peace untouched. If general war is not necessarily inevitable, as perhaps it was not very long ago, the pressures that underlie war are still with us. They are capable of breaking out with dangerous violence, as in the Near East and Eastern Europe. They may be far harder to contain under a policy of renunciation of force.

This brings the wheel around full-circle. If all-out war has been outlawed by the overmastering facts of life, rather than by fiat or treaty, something is needed in its place — a means of change without war. But this is needed not only because the "law" suffers from an unfortunate "gap." It is needed because there has been no outlawry of human nature, of political interests, of social dynamics, or of the willingness of men in the final analysis to fight against odds for their deepest values.

The will of the *status quo* states is an insufficient and unsatisfactory general substitute for war. The will of the revolutionaries is an intolerable one. A factual situation in which war is actually not in the rational interest of states, must be created and nourished. To do this, a surrogate for war will have to possess the will and the necessary power, however organized. It will have to convince all parties that there is sufficient flexibility in the situation to move around, to make working settlements, and above all to change the "law" when such change is legitimately called for. In this setting, but only in this setting, "voting . . . provides a moral substitute for war." [16] This is the ideal, yet it is also the central fact about our political world that the past and the present can teach us about the United Nations and its future.

That future can not and will not be static. The laws of political physics will still operate. As pressures are contained by a real fear of war on all sides, those pressures will increase for changes to take place without war. The threat of force, however illegal, will still be present. Injustices will still be perpetuated, and irrationality will still pervade an important sector of human motivation. But political evolutions and transformations will have a measurably greater chance of taking place peacefully, as the alternatives become increasingly unacceptable.

PEACEFUL CHANGE
AND THE LEAGUE OF NATIONS

Indeed if great enmities are ever to be really settled, we think it will be, not by the system of revenge and military success, and by forcing an opponent to swear to a treaty to his disadvantage, but when the more fortunate combatant waives these his privileges, to be guided by gentler feelings, conquers his rival in generosity, and accords peace on more moderate conditions than he expected. —

Thucydides, *The Peloponnesian War*

Chapter 2

Peaceful Change in the League of Nations Covenant

Article 19: The Assembly may from time to time advise the reconsideration by Members of the League of treaties which have become inapplicable and the consideration of international conditions whose continuance might endanger the peace of the world. —

League of Nations Covenant

The several approaches taken by the powers during the First World War with respect to postwar international organization varied with the differences in their historical traditions and strategic positions.

Inclined by its history to pragmatic, *ad hoc* solutions for the perennial outcroppings of political danger on the continent, Great Britain believed that its special insular position called for continuous action by the great powers, sometimes singly and sometimes in collaboration, to ameliorate disturbances to the *status quo*. In such collaborative arrangements Britain invariably retained sufficient flexibility so that diplomacy could forfend the development of an overwhelming combination of power across the Channel. If the danger materialized, Britain wanted freedom of choice to bring to bear the diplomatic and strategic techniques that its special situation had long since required it to perfect.

France was preoccupied with the growing inferiority of its position vis-à-vis Germany. Even in the midst of a war in which ultimate military triumph was guaranteed by American participation, France's impulses of statecraft were so focused on international guarantees against German recrudescence that all other considerations were secondary.

Italy had failed, in exchange for 600,000 lives, to take decisive possession of any more than 9,000 square miles of the Austro-Hungarian residue on the Adriatic for which she had entered the war. President Wilson utterly rejected the secret Treaty of London which in 1915 had guaranteed to Italy the now undelivered spoils. So Italy found itself deprived of its booty, shamed by an inferior military performance, saddled with debt, ruled over by a weak government, and, in general, gravely demoralized.

The United States presented a special case. Inexperience and deliberate unfamiliarity with world politics put this country at a great intellectual disadvantage, but it also provided certain political advantages. Unburdened by a sophisticated sense of its enduring interest with respect to Europe, this nation was able to transcend the intellectual boundaries that a keen historical awareness might have otherwise imposed. American statesmen felt free to experiment with novel political notions, some of which ultimately prevailed with the formation of the League of Nations.

THE DRAFTING OF ARTICLE 19

Against this background, the notion of peaceful change took shape in the League Covenant. It was never fully conceived or comprehended. It was a minor factor by comparison with the primary concerns of the League: enforcement, disarmament, and pacific settlement of disputes. It was thought of chiefly in connection with the revision of treaties. But it was a beginning.

On January 18, 1918, President Wilson had enunciated his Fourteen Points. The last of these, calling for the creation of a "general association of nations," described its essential purpose as "affording mutual guarantees of political independence and territorial integrity to great and small states alike." [1]

The Allied governments, in response, began to outline their ideas for institutionalizing such a guarantee. The first governmental text for a Covenant was prepared by the British Committee on the League of Nations under the direction of Lord Phillimore. It made no reference to treaty revision or change, except perhaps in the recognition that arbitration was a good way to settle disputes.[2]

A committee established by the French government under former Premier Leon Bourgeois prepared a plan which had little effect on official thinking, resting as it did on the need for international military forces under a permanent international staff.[3] Premier Clemenceau simply disregarded it when the Paris Peace Conference began.

The Italian government offered a rather remarkable plan which was never seriously discussed. The starting point was "international equity." A judiciary would have the task of interpreting existing law, but an international legislature would have the job of changing that law, with the power to make absolute decisions. The League would guarantee to all political communities not their territorial integrity or political independence, but their "growth." Machinery would be set up to control international distribution of raw materials. The keynote was "international social justice." [4] This display of flexibility, it need scarcely be pointed out, reflected Italy's highly unfavorable position at the close of the war.

President Wilson turned to his confidant, Colonel E. M. House, to prepare an American draft. On January 16, 1918, House presented his chief with a draft. The House plan, unlike its French and British counterparts, addressed itself decisively to the problem of peaceful change. Article 20 began with the principle of guarantees which later became Article 10 of the Covenant, standing at the heart of the subsequent conception of the League as a security agency for the insurance of the European order of 1919 against attack. But to make these guarantees unqualified would be to freeze that order *in perpetuo*.

To resolve this dilemma, Colonel House used as his catalyst the principle of self-determination which also was at the center of the Wilsonian outlook.[5] He produced a synthesis that carried the notion of peaceful change, in a constitutional context, further than it has since traveled even to this day:

> The Contracting Powers unite in several guarantees to each other of their territorial integrity and political independence subject, however, to such territorial modifications, if any, as may become necessary in the future by reason of changes in present racial conditions and aspirations, pursuant to the principle of self-determination, and as shall also be regarded by three fourths of the Delegates as necessary and proper for the welfare of the peoples concerned; recognizing also that all territorial changes involve equitable compensation and that the peace of the world is superior in importance and interest to questions of boundary.[6]

That final element of "compensation" characterized the sort of traditional diplomacy Wilson persistently repudiated, and evoked an age of Balance of Power politics that he persistently deplored. And yet it was an integral part of this scheme. House's idea was perhaps vague and it was obviously unrealistic for its day. Nonetheless, it revealed a dawning consciousness that the new League would have to function in a world of dynamic forces that would require continuous adjustment and compromise. Colonel House explained to the President in his letter of transmittal:

> No. 20 was written with the thought that it would not do to have territorial guarantees inflexible. It is quite conceivable that conditions might so change in the course of time as to make it a serious hardship for certain portions of one nation to continue under the government of that nation. For instance, it is conceivable that Canada might sometime wish to become part of the United States. It is also a possibility that Chihuahua, Coahuila or Lower California might desire to become a part of this country and with the consent in each instance of the mother country.[7]

President Wilson toyed with this revolutionary idea, and in his own first draft retained it almost verbatim.[8] After reaching Paris to attend the Peace Conference, Wilson revised his draft, chiefly along the lines suggested by the lengthy memorandum from Marshal Smuts which lay before the delegates. But he left this section unchanged, and was reported as saying that the guarantees were to be subject to

> . . . later alteration of terms and alteration of boundaries if it could be shown that injustice had been done or that conditions had changed. Any such alteration would be the easier to make in time as passion subsided and matters could be viewed in the light of justice rather than in the light of a peace conference at the close of a protracted war.[9]

David Hunter Miller, legal adviser to the United States Delegation, strongly urged the deletion of any provisions weakening the guarantees. His point of view toward peaceful change would be heard with increasing frequency from France and the successor states of the Hapsburg empire, as they saw the guarantees lose meaning: "Such general provisions," Miller cautioned, ". . . will make . . . dissatisfaction permanent, will compel every Power to engage in propaganda and will legalize irredentist agitation in at least all of Eastern Europe."[10]

Nonetheless, the earlier language appeared again in Wilson's Second Paris Draft of January 20, 1919.[11]

The roles of the United States and Great Britain underwent a curious reversal in the negotiations that followed. The British delegation, while still critical of the original American "peaceful change" proposal as an excessive intrusion on sovereignty, was alarmed at the rigidity its own stand would impart to the conduct of British foreign policy, and pressed to make the guarantees more flexible. Meanwhile the Americans, perhaps more responsive to the importunities of France, were backing away from the notion of peaceful change in the Covenant.

The British Draft Convention of January 20, 1919, was a novel attempt to surmount these difficulties. It suggested this paragraph to follow the territorial guarantees:

If at any time it should appear that the boundaries of any State guaranteed by Art. 1(1)(ii) do not conform to the requirements of the situation, the League shall take the matter under consideration and may recommend to the parties affected any modification which it may think necessary. If such recommendation is rejected by the parties affected, the States members of the League, shall, so far as the territory in question is concerned, cease to be under the obligation to protect the territory in question from forcible aggression by other States, imposed upon them by the above provision.[12]

This was interesting for three reasons. First, as a separate paragraph, it left the guarantees to stand by themselves. Second, by presupposing that the territorial guarantees would be crucial to the working of the League, it, third, suggested a way around the dilemma of enforcing territorial change, by the negative solution of withdrawing the guarantee, thus permitting the traditional processes of forcible change.

But Miller deplored this British loosening of the guarantees as much as he had deplored the American attempt. He urged Lord Cecil, as he had urged Wilson, to drop the idea of territorial modification and consider instead a program of protection of minorities.[13] In the draft which Cecil and Miller jointly prepared on January 27, 1919, still another paragraph was appended to the territorial guarantee in an effort to meet both points of view:

In considering any such modification the League shall take into account changes in the present conditions and aspirations of peoples or present social and political relations, pursuant to the principle, which the High Contracting Parties accept without reservation, that Governments derive their just powers from the consent of the governed.[14]

But in the Hurst-Miller draft which followed, both paragraphs following the territorial guarantee were deleted. President Wilson, for reasons that have never been fully spelled out, concurred.[15]

The guarantees were thus left to stand alone, without qualification. Why did Wilson accept this in the face of his earlier conviction as to the need for flexibility? A recent historian of the League writes that it was "the passionate anxiety of the French to maintain the sacred and unchangeable character of the Versailles settlement." [16] Another report was that the notion of peaceful change had vanished at this point because it was considered "too full of loopholes to survive close scrutiny." [17]

What was clear, however, was that the Covenant was now equipped with a guarantee of perpetual duration for the *status quo* of Versailles which neither British nor American leadership had particularly intended. So, at the Fourth meeting of the Commission of February 6, 1919, Lord Cecil proposed adding to the territorial guarantee the following words:

> Subject, however, to provision being made by the Body of Delegates for the periodic revision of treaties which have become obsolete and of international conditions, the continuance of which may endanger the peace of the world.[18]

President Wilson, according to Miller, "expressed the opinion that the provision could go through the Senate." [19]

At the meeting on February 11, the question arose whether the League Assembly would have power to revise treaties. According to the Czechoslovak delegate, if "the Assembly were to become the judge of all treaties it would have powers like those of an international parliament." [20] Confronted with this specter, the delegates readily agreed to Wilson's proposal of a new separate article:

> It shall be the right of the Body of Delegates from time to time to advise the reconsideration by the States, members of the League, of treaties which have become inapplicable, and of

international conditions, the continuance of which may endanger the peace of the world.[21]

With very little further discussion, this became Article 19 of the Covenant.

Wilson's formula, although superficially similar to Cecil's proposal, was different in one crucial respect: it limited the Assembly to advising the reconsideration *by the States themselves* "of treaties which have become inapplicable."

One later view was that the British language was "deliberately changed" in order to make it acceptable to both the revisionists and the champions of the *status quo*.[22] This was amplified by Harold Nicolson, who wrote in his memoirs of the Peace Conference:

> It is impossible to estimate how many decisions were accepted, how often obstruction was relinquished, how frequently errors were passed over, under the aegis of that blessed Article XIX . . . I am convinced that practically all of President Wilson's own backslidings were justified in his own conscience by the thought that "The Covenant will put that right." [23]

Both Lloyd George and President Wilson, said Nicolson, saw the new provision as "an escape from their misfortunes," and never really faced up to the ambivalent purposes of the League in looking backward to the Versailles Treaty on the one hand, and forward to Article 19 on the other.[24]

Italy, the only one of The Four to advocate a dynamic and revisionist program at Paris, was not only dealing from weakness, but was already on the descent into an attitude of hostility to the *status quo* as a whole.

THE ESTABLISHED ORDER VERSUS ARTICLE 19

At the Peace Conference the distance between the positions of the French and Italian delegates was the distance between the *status quo* and burgeoning revolution. Devotion to the order established at Paris was in direct proportion to the stake a nation had in the *status quo* — France, for example. The far different impulse to have guaranteed, not territorial integrity but justice and growth, was in direct proportion to dissatisfaction with the allocation of benefits, power, and "honor" to a nation — Italy, for example.

Somewhere between those two poles the United States was a free neutron, so to speak, bombarding first one fixed atom and then the other. It acted out the role of a power that believed itself free of enduring ties to the established political and strategic order, experimenting one day with notions of change, the next day retreating to a more conservative position.

The League, conceived in unavoidable compromise, contained the inherent contradictions of any inventive social experiment. Such peace-keeping machinery as the nations did agree to in the Covenant was necessarily at the disposal of the powers with the greatest stake in maintaining the territorial *status quo* in Europe, as well as Africa and Asia, where colonies had changed hands. The power positions had been defined by 1919, and were codified in the Treaty of Versailles, whose territorial dispositions were in turn firmly guaranteed by Article 10 of the Covenant.

Yet at least some of the delegates honestly believed that in Article 19 they had somehow ensured that the *status quo* could legally be altered if injustices or changed conditions intervened.

In the face of the real strategic situation of 1919 and the decade that followed, these left-handed efforts to append to the basic guarantees some vague provisions to sponsor, by a "democratic" process, alterations in the *status quo*, could only be meaningless.

Chapter 3

The Return of Violent Change

Man has much more to fear from the passions of his fellow-creatures than from the convulsions of the elements. —

Edward Gibbon, *The Decline and Fall of the Roman Empire*

On September 10, 1931, Viscount Cecil, in a classic example of history's "famous last words," told the League of Nations Assembly that "there has scarcely ever been a period in the world's history when war seemed less likely than it does at present." [1] Eight days later Japan attacked Manchuria, and a month later the last important country to adhere to traditional principles of free trade — Great Britain — took the first step toward the introduction of a general tariff.

This is not the place to develop a comprehensive recital of the events that unfolded like a Greek tragedy throughout the twenties and thirties until the final acts of violence and tragedy.[2] But some historic landmarks have special relevance, particularly certain provisions of the peace treaties. The peace treaties are important because the notion of peaceful change in the interwar years revolved almost exclusively around the idea of treaty revision. For the Germans, the *Diktat* of Versailles furnished both the symbol and the tangible target of revisionary sentiment throughout the entire period between the two wars.

These factors will suffice for our story, with the clear understanding that to account for the malignant growth of totalitarian and militaristic societies, we should properly give equal attention to the economic policies of the victors toward

Germany, the crisis of confidence and morale in Italy, and the economic and demographic pressures within Japan.

THE PEACE SETTLEMENT BECOMES THE STATUS QUO

The armistice agreement which Germany signed on November 11, 1918, included in its text not only the Fourteen Points, but also the additional principles President Wilson had enunciated in his various public pronouncements. It thus embodied the policies of self-determination, no secret agreements, no annexation, satisfaction of well-defined national aspirations, and impartial justice.[3]

Despite these hortatory directives, Germany was stripped of her colonies in Africa and the Pacific. Point Five may have spoken of "a free, open-minded and absolutely impartial adjustment of colonial claims," but no statesman who proposed returning Germany's colonies could have survived politically.

In Europe, while France could not get Allied agreement to French control of the left bank of the Rhine and annexation of the Saar Basin, Germany did retrocede Alsace-Lorraine to France, and Eupen and Malmedy to Belgium. The Saar was placed under international administration, with French economic hegemony, until the 1935 plebiscite. Posen and West Prussia were given to Poland, Danzig became a free state, Memel reverted to the Allies for disposition, and French military occupation was established on the left bank of the Rhine for fifteen years, with a demilitarized zone extending fifty kilometers into Germany.

As to reparations, Germany was required to pay for all civilian damage caused by the war, starting with five billion dollars, the rest to be paid over thirty years. The German Army was permanently limited to 100,000 men and the German Navy limited to six warships, with submarines and military aircraft unconditionally banned.

Left in dispute or to be settled by plebiscites were most of Schleswig, as well as East Prussia and Upper Silesia. Finally, by Article 231 of the Armistice agreement, Germany assumed the burden of war guilt:

> The Allied and Associated Governments affirm and Germany accepts the responsibility of Germany and her allies for causing all the loss and damage to which the Allied and Associated Governments and their nationals have been subjected as a consequence of the war imposed upon them by the aggression of Germany and her allies.[4]

This, then, was the *Diktat* of Versailles. With it Adolf Hitler was to create for the German people the greatest mass persecution complex in history, and, at least for a time, the greatest guilt complex in history on the part of those who had imposed it.

The problems confronting Italy have been cited briefly. Japan had entered the peace conference with two paramount objectives, and emerged with a low final score. She failed, among other things, to get explicit recognition in the League Covenant of the principle of the equality of races (a wound that bled profusely again only five years later with the passage of the Immigration and Naturalization Act by the United States Congress). And, while President Wilson reluctantly acceded to the Japanese claim to the former German territory on China's Shantung Peninsula in order to keep Japan in the peace conference, combined American and British pressure at the Washington Conference only three years later forced Japan to yield it up again.

The years 1919–1935 saw the rise, the hegemony, and the decline of French political domination of Europe. France's position in 1924 has been described as comparable to Metternich's Austria in 1815, having reached the summit of its power and prestige in Europe and playing the role of champion of the *status quo* and sworn enemy of revisionism. Others have seen it as analogous to the Quadruple Alliance vis-à-vis post-Napoleonic France, in that the Little Entente, for example, was aimed exclusively against revival of Germany's international position.[5]

It is generally supposed by historians that France might have felt secure enough to go along with a positive program of German rehabilitation if the United States had agreed to the treaty of guarantee that was to accompany the Versailles Treaty, or even if the United States had signed the Versailles Treaty and become a member of the League. But as it was, France called the turns to the extent that no projects for disarmament, for economic concessions, and above all for territorial adjustments had a chance without her consent. The endless circular debates in and out of the League between arms and security, between *rapprochement* and guarantees, and between French logic and French fears, seemed only to enhance the attachment of French policy to the *status quo* of 1919 with respect to the relative positions of France and Germany.

The circularity of the problem was illustrated by the fate of the 1924 Geneva *Protocol for the Pacific Settlement of International Disputes*. While the League Covenant, in its collective security provisions, had revived the concept of *bellum justum* — the legitimate, police-type war — it retreated in Article 12 to a position of moral neutrality, requiring only a token waiting period before a nation in certain circumstances could legally resort to war. The Geneva Protocol aimed at closing this gap by requiring the Council to refer disputes that were not otherwise settled, to a committee of arbitrators who would have binding powers of decision.

But the report submitted to the Fifth League Assembly on the Protocol clearly stipulated that a demand for revision of a treaty provision was *not* a "dispute" within the meaning of the Protocol:

There is a third class of disputes to which the new system of pacific settlement can also not be applied. These are disputes which aim at revising treaties and international acts in force, or which seek to jeopardize the existing territorial integrity of signatory states. The proposal was made to include these exceptions in the Protocol, but the two committees [the report was submitted on behalf of the First and Third Committees. LPB] were unanimous in considering that, both from the legal and political point of view, the impossibility of applying compulsory arbitration to such cases was so obvious that it was quite superfluous to make them the subject of a special provision. It was thought sufficient to mention them in this report.[6]

The Protocol thus identified security with the maintenance of the territorial provisions of 1919, and there was still no machinery for their revision. And the British Commonwealth for its own reasons killed it by refusing to ratify.

"Those nations which dominated the League — the victors of the World War — " John Foster Dulles wrote in 1939, "conceived the League primarily as an instrumentality for perpetuating the status quo . . . they conceived of peace as the avoidance of all change." They placed great emphasis on the guarantees contained in Article 10, and on the collective security measures of Article 16 in defense of those guarantees, but "no thought was given to setting up machinery to effect changes from time to time in those treaties and in those international conditions" envisaged by Article 19. Under French domination, Dulles continued, the Covenant became an alliance to maintain the unchanging status of the ex-enemy states, under the slogan of sanctity of treaties. Those seeking changes were branded as potential aggressors.[7]

THE CLAIMS AGAINST THE STATUS QUO

The "potential aggressors" had some slogans of their own. "Sanctity of treaties" had its counterpart, not in the legal doctrine of *rebus sic stantibus* but in the doctrine of the "scrap of paper." A favorite slogan was "a place in the sun." Others were more meaningful: *Lebensraum*, *Italia Irredenta*,

Co-Prosperity Sphere — symbols reflecting both the rigidity of the post-Versailles order and the mounting fanaticism of the discontented states.

The most significant meeting in that earlier era of "summit conferences" was not between Hitler and Chamberlain. It was between two intangible forces. There was a point, somewhere in the period, at which the growing loss of confidence and nerve among the Western victors collided in time and space with, and was overtaken by the *élan vital* of the vanquished. The latter, in their sense of betrayal and failure, had consumed their own stabilizing centers. They had filled the resulting void with a new secular religion, complete with a gospel of national destiny, a pathological demonology, and the godhead of the hypostasized state.

The so-called expansionist powers [8] avoided debating issues according to the logic of the value systems they opposed, for this would have betrayed the profound irrationality of their doctrines. But some of the leaders had their own cynical rationale, candidly exposed to the Nürnberg Tribunal by Hjalmar Schacht:

> I think you can score many more successes when you want to lead someone if you don't tell them the truth than if you tell them the truth.[9]

So, when the claims were not keyed exclusively to the iniquities of the Versailles *Diktat* and the compulsive need for revenge, arguments were advanced that were superficially rational, oriented to values the democracies could understand and even respect. Thus the dissenters spoke of the need for greater access to raw materials and markets for the disposal of surplus manufactures, the need for relief from population pressures, and the difficulty of securing foreign exchange, to justify the return of Germany's colonies, the expansion of Italy's African empire, and Japan's economic, political, and cultural penetration into the Asiatic mainland.

John Stuart Mill once wrote:

> It is a rule both of justice and of good sense to grapple not with the absurdest, but with the most reasonable form of a wrong opinion.[10]

In this spirit some Anglo-Saxon leaders took very seriously the clamant cries of the dissenting powers. But they remained skeptical of the rational grounds behind those claims. No one could deny that Germany, Italy, and Japan were convulsed by a frightful economic depression, but clearly everyone was in the same boat. As to population pressures, Belgium, the United Kingdom, and the Netherlands were higher up on the list than Germany, according to any reliable index of relative density.[11] Germany had more arable land *per capita* than Switzerland or Czechoslovakia. Belgium, Holland, China, and India had the same problem of arable land as Japan. Czechoslovakia and the Scandinavian countries were resource-poor like the Axis powers. Latin America, which rarely spoke of *lebensraum* or colonies, was as shy of coal as Italy.

Colonies were manifestly not being used to absorb surplus populations: by 1914 less than 20,000 Germans had colonized territories they held for twenty years. The Japanese population had multiplied by one million a year, yet in an entire generation less than half a million Japanese migrated to Korea and Manchuria. As for colonies as export markets, the *per capita* purchasing capacity of the typical native of a former German African colony was fantastically low, and in fact German trade with its colonies in 1914 was less than 1 per cent of its total world trade. The alleged currency difficulties encountered in purchasing raw materials really represented a question of tariffs which could be negotiated, or so it was argued.

All in all, it was generally agreed that none of these factors by themselves made much sense except in a pattern of economic self-sufficiency. Then it was simple to demolish the arguments by attacking the basic premise of autarky. In a setting of free trade there would be comparatively few advantages, in terms of real income, from the acquisition of legal sovereignty over the disputed colonies.[12]

Still, the grievances were not imaginary, and the setting did not happen to be one of free trade. The League of Nations organized a Committee on Raw Materials which, while ruling out the transfer of colonies, investigated the question of "equality of access" to raw materials. The League itself took certain steps toward removal of export restrictions. Some writers, seeing this as a strategic avenue to solution of the larger political difficulties, urged greater generosity on the part of the "satisfied" powers, citing the provisions of the 1885 General Act of Berlin regarding the Congo Basin as the model for a new "open door policy" in all colonial areas.[13]

But there had to be more intelligible claims behind this economic façade. Frederick S. Dunn was among the few to identify some of them in the idiom of power. The configurations of power relationships, he reasoned, had changed, and those on the short end were driven to restore the *status quo ante*. The factor of prestige was closely related to the power drive, and displayed itself irrationally, as when Benito Mussolini announced that he was compelled to take Ethiopia by force as a "demonstration." The factor of national honor was linked to the others. Ethnic unity was a variable that can either be brought to white heat or kept cool, depending on the manipulative techniques involved. So far as the drive for self-sufficiency was concerned, in retrospect it indicated preparation for war and could be made explicable only in those terms.[14]

Given this discrepancy between the verbal arguments on the one hand and the political and sociological realities on the other, simply to unmask the Axis claims as irrational had no effect at all on the tensions that underlay them.[15] While the struggle of the Japanese militarists for control was not completely resolved until the mid-thirties, surely the regimes in Germany and Italy passed the point of no return considerably earlier.

If this is a correct diagnosis, it explains why recourse was never had by the aggrieved powers to Article 19 of the Covenant as a lever to pry open the Versailles settlement for the benefit of Germany, or to revise other phases of the existing political and legal order for the satisfaction of Italy and Japan.[16] The grievances of the three accumulated to a point where they could be satisfied only at the overwhelming expense of those still ascendant, if indeed at all.

THE LESSON OF HISTORY

If the German, Italian, and Japanese claims had been given serious and mature attention at Paris in 1919, would history have been different? Would an early and generous reconciliation have produced better results than the later varieties of appeasement?

History has shown a certain tendency to repeat itself after major wars that are followed by territorial settlements. Such situations involve a gainer and a loser. If the settlement is unpalatable to the loser, unless he is destroyed, as for example Rome ultimately came to be, he generally strains to place himself in a position strong enough to challenge the settlement.

The egregious modern example is the series of postwar oscillations between France and Germany. From earlier ages French-English relations stand out, and other examples go back to the protracted duel between Athens and Sparta. Even where *irredentist* territory was not at stake, nations were often spurred to frenzies of recovery by motives involving national honor, vengeance, power-hunger, or the need for national self-assertion.

Against this background, the chief lesson of 1919 was one

of timing. Starting from the moment of settlement, the possibility of rectifying a bad initial situation without having to undergo the characteristic ordeal, seemed to diminish with the square root of the distance away from that moment, like the intensity of light. As time elapsed, the power of rational choice and purposeful action increasingly eluded the victors who, still debauched with their victories, watched helplessly as the structure of peace disintegrated.

It is not necessary to say, with Pope, "Whatever is, is right." Men and nations must endure the judgments of history. But while an unfair or draconian peace settlement is invariably a grave error for which the full price must ultimately be paid, one must always ask whether radically different choices were open at the time.

There are times when an error must be made because action is confined within the limits set by time, space, and the stage of a people's development. The United States, for example, was "being itself" when an emotionally unprepared Senate voted down the League of Nations Covenant (and when American troops were brought home in 1945). This view can be called deterministic only in that it accepts as the capability of an organism, human or social, that of which it is presently capable. This does not define its potentialities nor does it rule out the capacity of new leadership and new ideas to reshape the social material.

But an international repair job is uphill all the way. Time is against the repairmen, as the peace settlement from which they have profited deteriorates. It is at the beginning of the cycle that human intelligence and initiative can be most creative.

In some extraordinary instances statesmanship can bring off a political miracle later in the process, as with the freeing of India in 1947, only a few years before a fatal revolution was bound to occur (or so it appears to one who knew the India of 1945). The British withdrawal and transfer of sovereignty was executed in sufficient time so that today the improbable has happened and, despite all the strains over colonial issues, British policy is highly respected by the government of India.

But one should not count on miracles. Action that is too little and too late is far more customary, and generally tantalizes the expanding power's appetite until it becomes positively voracious.

To the question, "Would timely action in the 1920's have changed the future?," one can say only that a little time was available even after Versailles. A liberal, democratic centrist regime went on to have its fleeting moment of destiny under the Weimar Republic. The struggle between moderates and militants in Japan was not finally resolved until the Taisho Emperor died in 1936. Benito Mussolini had been a socialist journalist before he became a fascist dictator. Perhaps there was time to have rewritten history.

But it is still speculative whether as time went on even a determined — and historically unprecedented — effort to evaluate rationally the basic claims of the dissenters would have reversed the course of events that were already in train. For as early as 1923 Adolf Hitler had written:

> The winning back of the lost territories is not achieved through solemn invocations of the Lord God or through pious hopes in a League of Nations, but through armed force.[17]

Chapter 4

The Fate of Article 19

> The great majority of mankind are satisfied with appearances, as though they were realities, and are often even more influenced by the things that seem than by those that are. —
>
> Niccolò Machiavelli, *Discourses*

Four disparate but related factors stand out in the picture so far: Woodrow Wilson's tentative insight into the problem of peaceful change; the invidious position of Article 19 in the light of the Versailles settlement; the estrangement of the fascist regimes from the community of victors in the League; and the apocalyptic vision of Adolf Hitler, which precluded application to either Heaven or Geneva for redress of Germany's grievances. The story of what actually happened to Article 19 gives the picture its final symmetry.

Article 19 was never once invoked by those who sought to revise the Versailles settlement, or in their behalf. In fact, it was never conclusively invoked with respect to any situation. It was, for all practical purposes, a dead letter before the ink was dry on the Covenant.

Article 19 was actually cited before the League Assembly in two cases. The first was a mild assault on the treaties Chile had imposed on Peru and Bolivia after the Pacific War of 1879–84. The second was an ambiguous attempt by the Chinese government, courteously phrased, to draw attention to the so-called "unequal treaties" which were still in force. The treatment accorded these two matters reflected faithfully the dilemma in the very concept of Article 19 which made it so improbable as an instrument of peaceful change. It also illustrated the Geneva atmosphere which itself tended to emasculate whatever potential for needful action may have existed at the core of Article 19.

THE BOLIVIAN-CHILEAN CASE

On November 1, 1920, Bolivia, whose provinces of Tacna and Arica were still occupied by Chile, formally invoked Article 19 "with a view to obtaining from the League of Nations the revision of the Treaty of Peace signed between Bolivia and Chile on October 20, 1904." The explanatory letter charged that the treaty had been imposed by force, certain of its fundamental articles had not been executed by Chile, and the resulting state of affairs "involves a permanent menace of war." Bolivia asked that the matter be placed on the agenda of the First Assembly.[1] Peru, likewise invoking Article 19 (as well as Article 15), asked the Assembly to "reconsider and revise" the Treaty with Chile of October 20, 1883, for essentially the same reasons. (It will be recalled that the drafters of the Covenant had expressly decided against empowering the Assembly itself to revise treaties.)

But when the Assembly convened in November of 1920, the two governments reported that they wished to examine the matter among themselves, and it was provisionally adjourned.[2] The Peruvian request was subsequently withdrawn. The Chilean delegation went on record that "neither the League . . . nor the Assembly can interfere,"[3] and there the matter rested until the following year. There is some evidence that France was influential in persuading Bolivia not to insist on pursuing this action at the 1920 session,[4] obviously having in mind the dangerous precedent such interference with an imposed treaty settlement would establish.

Bolivia had meanwhile reserved the right to reopen this issue, and the next year requested that its appeal be heard.

Chile remained "absolutely opposed," asserting that the "League was absolutely and radically incompetent to revise treaties, especially treaties of peace." [5]

On September 15, 1921, the General Committee of the Assembly, with Chile's blessing, decided to invite three jurists, members of the Assembly, "to give their joint opinion on the powers of the Assembly, under Article 19." [6] Messrs. Scialoja (Italy), Urrutia (Colombia), and de Peralta (Costa Rica) in two weeks produced an opinion that is worth quoting in full:

> That, in its present form, the request of Bolivia is not in order, because the Assembly. . . cannot of itself modify any treaty, the modification of treaties lying solely within the competence of the . . . States;
>
> That the Covenant, while insisting on scrupulous respect for all treaty obligations in the dealings of organized peoples with one another, by Article 19 confers on the Assembly the power to advise the consideration by Members . . . of certain treaties or the consideration of certain international conditions;
>
> That such advice can only be given in cases where treaties have become inapplicable — that is to say, when the state of affairs existing at the moment of their conclusion has subsequently undergone, either materially or morally, such radical changes that their application has ceased to be reasonably possible, or in cases of the existence of international conditions whose continuance might endanger the peace of the world;
>
> That the Assembly would have to ascertain, if a case arose, whether one of these conditions did in point of fact exist.[7]

In thus finessing with a technicality a potentially embarrassing action, the Committee not unexpectedly rested its interpretation of Article 19 on juridical grounds that might be taken for a restatement of the doctrine of *rebus sic stantibus*, paying as it did only passing tribute to the second of Article 19's conditions — the strictly political criterion of "international conditions whose continuance might endanger the peace of the world." Even here, the context supported the inference that no collective action of this sort was possible until the trouble became sufficiently explosive as to be irremediable.

Bolivia (and needless to say, Chile) accepted this ambiguous finding, insisting as an afterthought that it had not asked the League to revise the treaty but had merely inquired whether the situation justified an invitation to the two states to undertake the process of reconsideration. Nonetheless, even though the Committee based its rejection of the claim on the technical question of form, Bolivia agreed not to persist and, reserving its right to bring it up still again, allowed the request to lapse. President Balfour termed the matter closed, and remanded to the parties.[8]

THE CHINESE TREATIES

The Chinese case, which assumed an even more equivocal shape, began at the Sixth Assembly in 1925 when the Chinese delegate adverted to his country's appeals to the powers for reconsideration of their treaty relations. (Under the unequal treaties of the nineteenth century these relations were still characterized by such features as capitulatory courts and extraterritoriality.) Only a few months earlier the British had used gunfire to disperse student demonstrations at Shanghai and Canton. China in retaliation boycotted British goods and shipping until the fall of 1936. But the Chinese delegate delicately refrained from discussing the substance of China's grievances, saying only "I bring this question before the Assembly because it is within the province of the letter and spirit of the Covenant of the League, particularly in Article 19." The treaties in question were "inapplicable and . . . not in harmony with international conditions in respect of China's position . . . There should be a readjustment of the existing treaties." He concluded that the League should congratulate itself for witnessing China's pioneering use of Article 19.[9]

The process of watering down an already mild complaint took place at once, and eight meetings later the Chinese delegate moved a resolution that read simply:

The Assembly, Having heard with deep interest the Chinese Delegate's suggestion regarding the possibility of considering, according to the spirit of the Covenant, the existing international conditions in China,

Having heard with satisfaction that a Conference of the interested States is soon to take place in China to consider the questions involved;

Expresses its hope that a satisfactory solution may be reached at an early date.[10]

He did, however, refer with some asperity to Article 19 and to the inapplicability of the treaties in question, concluding hopefully "we all recognize that Article 19 of the Covenant is a remedy for changing international conditions which endanger the peace of the world." His resolution was adopted.[11]

Two years later Persia unilaterally denounced the system of capitulations imposed by the Western powers, and in 1928 China followed suit. Also in 1928 treaties were concluded by China with twelve states which agreed to recognize the Nanking government and its right to complete tariff autonomy. By 1930 nine nationalities had lost their extraterritorial privileges in China, and several more had agreed to their termination when the practice became universally abolished. Nevertheless, by 1939, extraterritorial privileges in China were still retained by the powers that mattered: France, Great Britain, Japan, and the United States.

So in 1929, when the Chinese Vice-President of the Assembly reopened the question of Article 19, China's grievances still rankled. Deploring the desuetude into which Article 19 had been permitted to lapse, he demanded to know why nothing had been done.[12]

Six days later he returned to the charge. With a nice sense of face-saving, he advanced the novel theory that "the Assembly really has not the time to consider the intricate questions which may come under this Article." He suggested that a committee be established to find the most effective means of making Article 19 operative.[13]

As the tenth session matured, support grew from the ranks of the discontented members of the League, such as Germany, India, Persia, Hungary, and Abyssinia, for the Chinese resolution, whose preamble read:

> The Assembly, Considering that Article 19 of the Covenant . . . is one of the most essential articles of the Covenant in the cause of international cooperation and peace;
>
> Observing that, nevertheless, it has not once been acted upon during the decade of the existence of the League;
>
> Believing that such inaction has been due to the fact that the Assembly has not had the necessary assistance and advice . . .

It repeated the recommendation that a committee be named "to consider and report on the best methods to make effective the above mentioned article." [14]

But a subcommittee including Great Britain and Belgium [15] on September 24 reported unfavorably on the creation of the proposed study committee, on the grounds that it was not desirable to give the impression that Article 19 was either inoperative, or needed to be restored or given greater effectiveness.

The subcommittee, noting that the question of applying Article 19 "has previously been studied" (presumably referring to the two-week effort by the Committee of Jurists in 1921), offered its own draft resolution which blandly declared:

> . . . that a Member of the League may, on its own responsibility . . . place on the agenda of the Assembly the question whether the Assembly should give advice as contemplated by Article 19 regarding the reconsideration of any treaty or treaties which such

Member considers to have become inapplicable or the consideration of international conditions the continuation of which might, in its opinion, endanger the peace of the world.

If drawn up in proper form, the request should be considered by the Assembly, which should, "if it thinks proper, give the advice requested." [16]

In the course of debate, Rumania, reflecting the attitude of France and its allies, sought assurances that Article 19 in no way interfered with Article 10. Likewise, Japan, Yugoslavia, Czechoslovakia, and Chile, for their own reasons, made sure the interpretation of Article 19 was strictly limited. Poland and Hungary reserved their positions, and the resolution was adopted.[17] The members of the League were now able to place a preliminary question on the agenda, and it may be inferred that the Muse of History, if she noticed this bold act at all, stifled a yawn with grave difficulty.

THE LEAGUE IN RETROSPECT

Such is the repertory of practice in the League under Article 19. Not once was it invoked by those who, considering its origins, should have benefited the most from it. No reference was ever made in its name to a treaty consummated after 1914. Austria, Hungary, Bulgaria, and Turkey, as well as Germany, were highly dissatisfied with the peace settlement but never made use of Article 19. The territorial issues that grew out of the peace settlement were on occasion dealt with by the League — issues such as the Saar, Danzig, the Polish Corridor, the South Tyrol, and Transylvania, not to mention the former German colonies, but never with reference to Article 19.

In the two cases where Article 19 was invoked, it was promptly submerged under a mass of procedural evasions and anodyne phrases, and in neither case did the Assembly come to grips with the substantive claims behind the complaints.

France was responsible for several devices to ensure that the animals were not going to be let out of the cage via Article 19. There was the interpretation of the Geneva Protocol of 1924 mentioned earlier, which exempted treaty revisions from the category of disputes envisaged under Article 12. A decade later France was assuring its allies, after signing the four-power pact of June 1933, with England, Italy, and Germany, that absolute unanimity, including the vote of the parties involved, was needed to give any legal effect to a vote under Article 19.[18]

There were those who pointed out that the 1929 resolution acknowledged, as the 1921 resolution had not, the predominantly political nature of action under Article 19. This was represented as absolving Article 19 of any similarity with the doctrine of *rebus sic stantibus*.[19]

The metaphysics of this argument were overshadowed by the political facts. The juridical doctrine on which the leadership of the League stood was *pacta sunt servanda*, with specific reference to the Versailles Treaty. The deep-seated claims of the dissident powers were never submitted to adjudication, but if they had been, the claimants would have been as handicapped inside the courtroom as they were outside. The defendants sat not only on their legal rights but on the territories as well. They were equipped to reinforce their legal rights under *pacta* with the equally time-tested doctrine of *occupatio*, if not *dominium* or even, in the case of the colonial empires, *imperium*.

The postwar legal order, comprehensively identified with the political regime set up by the victorious powers, concentrated its attention on issues which were ostensibly based on claims involving legal rights:

> To this end, steps were taken toward strengthening the habit of law observance among nations, establishing adequate judicial machinery for deciding claims of legal right, improving and extending the scope of international law, and guaranteeing the

preservation of the status quo by the collective action of the international community. The general assumption underlying these moves was that the problem of war and peace was essentially one of protecting legal rights against potential lawbreakers.[20]

But the dangerous disputes turned out to be of the other kind: claims based, not on legal right, not on efforts to have a nation's share in the existing distribution of rights confirmed and protected, but on the "right" of nations, outside the scope of the legal order, to change the *status quo* itself.

If it was to function rationally, the League needed to operate in accordance with its real purposes. Its machinery was set up for the primary purpose of maintaining the *status quo*, and it could theoretically have so functioned, much as the Concert of Europe had somethimes functioned in the nineteenth century. If the major powers in the League had been willing to implement their own long-term policies, they would have aborted the tentative and, at first, unauthorized Japanese thrust into Manchuria in 1931, the small-scale German reoccupation of the Rhineland, and the movement of the Italian legions toward the Ethiopian adventure, as Winston Churchill, for one, consistently urged.

It is commonly asserted today and with good reason, that general war is unthinkable. But, looking back, it is hard to escape the conclusion that war, in 1939, was the only remaining course to be followed by two antagonistic, and, for different reasons, bankrupt policies. Preventive action by the West would have run the risk, however minimal, of general war. But the Western powers were consistently unwilling to run this risk until they finally had no choice, with the odds gravely against them, even though to carry out policies that were not only morally right but strategically correct demanded that willingness. As it was, the powers would neither hold on nor let go. The League was their instrument for maintenance of the *status quo*, but it was not so used. Yet neither was it allowed to entertain claims against the *status quo.*

Of course, even if a decisive course had been pursued, the problem would have been only half-solved. War or, conversely, the averting of war constitutes a start of policy, not a finish. Once the iron grip of totalitarianism had been relaxed and the timetable of its internal pathology upset, opportunities would have opened for generous and far-sighted economic policies and political programs to alleviate the continuing problem of the Axis countries, and to terminate their sense of alienation from the community of democratic nations. To convert such loosening of the situation into a new regime of stability would have taken wise and bold statesmanship.

This brand of statesmanship, even if it had ever really existed outside the minds of theorists, was in increasingly short supply as the need for it multiplied. As it was, the established order yielded neither enlightened justice on the one hand, nor the will to suppress its revolutionaries on the other. In the face of great power policy that had become confused and ambiguous, international organization became a symbol of impotence, feeding itself and its members on a diet of shame, guilt, and futility.

There is no theoretical obstacle to an international organization which protects the *status quo* as a rooted political value structure that has survived because it is good, but which also ameliorates that *status quo* for the benefit of the dissident minority groups that always split away from societies like parts of an amoeba. But this policy is insuperably difficult if the organization is controlled by powers that confuse possession with law, insist on policies because the policies are theirs, not because they are good, disagree as to just what *status quo* they are interested in protecting, and lack the will and nerve to act on a sense of their own vital interests.

In 1931 the Mukden Incident foreboded eventual Japanese

occupation of Manchuria. In 1932 Japan invested Shanghai and by 1937 was ready to invade China as a whole. In 1933 Germany withdrew from the League and in a fifteen-month period beginning in March 1935, not only formally and openly denounced the Versailles Treaty, but also the Locarno Pacts which only ten years previously had been freely negotiated and signed. Germany reoccupied the Rhineland. In the same span of time Italy invaded and annexed Ethiopia, a fellow member of the League.

This overturn of the order of things established at Paris in 1919, this "return to power politics," deplored with such good reason by so many people, marked, as E. H. Carr wrote in 1939, "the termination of the monopoly of power enjoyed by the *status quo* Powers."[21] The end of that monopoly prompted an outpouring of soul-searching analysis by participants and observers of international affairs who sought ways to meet, understand, and live with this phenomenon. To that effort, which revolved around the concept of peaceful change in a very special historical setting, we now turn.

Chapter 5

The 1930's: Peaceful Change Becomes an Issue

> [Democratic governments] are expected to arrest the evil when it breaks out, and yet they are asked to foster it whilst it is hatching. —
>
> François Guizot, *Democracy in France*

This chapter chronicles the search of scholars and statesmen in the middle 1930's for an escape route from the blind alley toward Armageddon in which the world seemed to be trapped. Their good intentions can be patronized only to the extent that our contemporary policies are designed to avoid the fate that befell theirs.

In another sense, it is the story of minds groping for the profound truths that are sometimes extruded in a crisis, when the broken shards of the accustomed order form themselves into a new and revelatory mosaic.

In a final sense it bespeaks the anguish of the intellectual when his society's Time of Troubles overtakes the rational mind's capacity to plan and execute reformatory action.

ARTICLE 19: A POSTSCRIPT

When the full extent of the revolution against the established order became apparent, some minds turned to Article 19 as a custom-made instrument for refashioning the collapsing territorial order. (It was generally agreed that the drafters of Article 19 had in mind chiefly, if not exclusively, the problem of territorial changes.[1])

John Foster Dulles was one of those who in the 1930's made a heroic effort to understand and, if possible, to repair the disintegrating structure of world peace. To him Article 19 represented, for the first time in history, the germ of an international authority with power to give or withhold moral sanction regarding treaties. As he saw it, Article 19 potentially combined the objective of avoiding violence, the means of periodic alterations of the *status quo* to balance dynamic against static forces, and the location of responsibility in an impartial body. Article 19, he concluded, was the real heart of the League — but it was a heart that never beat.[2]

"Many loyal and disinterested supporters of the League had long believed that (in Article 19) lay the chief defect of the Covenant, or at least of its application in actual practice," according to the League's most recent historian.[3] In the same vein a British statesman said of Article 19: "its inefficacy . . . reflects by far the greatest weakness of the League," and he recommended, just as his government had in January 1919, that

> . . . a country which . . . refused to give effect to the League's recommendation for a change in the status quo should thereby be deprived of its right to protection under the Covenant against a resulting war.[4]

Article 19, according to another English authority, envisaged not a legal operation but an appeal to public opinion. It "enshrines a principle (that) no arrangement of the world is sacred for all time." Unfortunately, there were no real means to make it effective and Article 19 must operate in silence, so to speak, through such alterations in the existing network of rights as the League Assembly's acceptance of the Report on Manchuria which was prepared under Article 15.[5]

Some saw Article 19 as a substitute for the classical method of the *fait accompli*.[6] To others it merely stated an unsolved problem, since those who wanted to use international law as an agency of change simply sought to mask the *fait accompli* "in the disguise of legal rectitude." Given the gradual *de facto* revision of the Versailles Treaty, taken alongside the two abortive Article 19 cases in the League Assembly, "the problem of peaceful change was reduced to its classic simplicity in any system of power politics: revision could be obtained by agreement, *fait accompli*, or war." [7]

The Registrar of the Permanent Court of International Justice saw in Article 19,

> . . . a notion of justice which is not the narrow notion of legal rights, but rather of a sort of immanent justice, the tangible expression of which is the maintenance of peace . . . the *dynamic* state of things.[8]

Why had it turned sour? Because of the requirement of unanimity, "statusquoism," the inconsistency of the revisionists, particularly their failure to amend or use Article 19, and finally the lack of legal and political authority to enforce changes brought about under Article 19. So wrote one scholar.[9]

The official post-mortem took place in Geneva in 1936, with the report of the Special Committee set up by the League "to study the application of the principles of the Covenant." In response to an invitation issued in 1936 for states to make proposals "to improve . . . the application of the principles of the Covenant," numerous suggestions were received, but curiously very few with respect to Article 19. In its support Australia commented:

> The League cannot succeed if it is to be turned into an instrument for the maintenance of the status quo at any given time. We must stand by the principle that the rule of law must also be the rule of equity.[10]

Great Britain freely acknowledged that human life was not static, and that the League failed when it imposed a stereotype of the *status quo*. Nevertheless, "it would plainly be impracticable . . . to seek to give the Assembly power to impose changes against the wish of the parties concerned." [11]

Bulgaria demanded that Article 19 be given a more flexible form, with provision for Assembly recommendations by less than unanimous vote. Hungary wanted the actionable conditions for the article's application to be clearly defined. Peru asked for greater Assembly authority, under a two-thirds majority rule. New Zealand suggested that all nations be invited to consider the peace treaties extant. Argentina, India, and Iraq made suggestions to strengthen Article 19.

But others recommended great caution in the application of Article 19. Portugal and the members of the Little Entente took the position that:

> . . . no change is possible without the free and formal consent of the parties concerned . . . to lay before the Assembly any territorial question, irrespective of the countries concerned, so far from serving the cause of peace, will seriously disturb good international understanding, on which peace depends.[12]

The Soviet Union, its post-revolutionary respect for the principle of absolute sovereignty growing steadily, concurred in this view.

The Special Committee, under the chairmanship of Maurice Bourquin of Belgium, made its report in 1938.

> Since Article 10 imposes an obligation on Members of the League to respect and preserve the territorial integrity of Members of the League, it is essential that States which put forward territorial claims should have peaceful machinery at their disposal to enforce those claims. This is the contingency for which Article 19 provides . . . (It) is an article providing for changes of an unusual character and of unquestionable seriousness; and, as such, it is not an article calling for constant application, so that the fact of its not having been enforced during a period of seventeen years after a time of extensive territorial changes has nothing abnormal about it.[13]

After thus satisfying itself that Article 19 had not been used because no "unusual" or "serious" problems had arisen between 1919 and 1937, the Committee went on to cite some changes that had been made in existing legal status, saying "if Article 19 has not been applied, its spirit has governed the changes in question." Trying one last tack, the Committee, acknowledging that the postwar territorial status had been opposed by "some," concluded:

It is a matter of regret . . . that Article 19 . . . which has not yet been applied, does not appear to be capable of bringing about a solution of certain political difficulties.[14]

Seven months later Czechoslovakia was, to all intents and purposes, liquidated, in defiance of Article 10, the Ten Commandments, and the self-interest of all the participants but one.

THE BACKGROUND OF THE DEBATE

Seven years before Munich, just after Japan attacked Manchuria, the opinion had developed, according to one writer, "that improvement in the means of 'peaceful change' was the only way in which war could be prevented."

. . . the victors of World War I, overinterested in the perpetuation of a particular *status quo*, had given inadequate attention to the development of procedures for peaceful change. Grievances providing fuel for those revolts against the international system had not been dealt with in time. It became clear that a working international polity must not only suppress aggression but must also prevent the development of political inferiority complexes.[15]

"Men," wrote another, "are seeking a way of escape from the catastrophe which the violent clash of . . . forces would make inevitable."[16]

John Foster Dulles spoke most unequivocally for those who were assuming on behalf of the *status quo* powers the burden of guilt for what had happened to world peace:

> Of course non-aggression and sanctity of treaties are *elements* of peace, but they are by no means its totality. Peace must also take account of the fact that life is essentially dynamic, that change is inevitable, and that transformations are bound to occur violently unless there are provided ways of peaceful change. Any world system is doomed if it identifies peace and morality with a mere maintenance of the *status quo*. To do this is to breed, as we have bred, the forces of revolution and revolt.[17]

Two other writers asked:

> Can peaceful methods be found to satisfy the demands of the dissatisfied nations? Is it possible to work out some intelligent method of meeting these problems? Can the answer be found in transferring territory, re-dividing land, or giving access to raw materials, or will this merely create new grievances and new inequalities? [18]

The greatly increased concern with the problem of peaceful change was interpreted in another way. People, it was said, generally feared war and were reluctant to face up to its implications. After 1935 Germany had already satisfied some of its long-standing claims. It was generally agreed that the Versailles settlement was unjust. It was recognized that economic advantages, easy to dispose of now that the whole world was economically in the same leaky boat, should have been shared when it might have turned the tide. But by the middle 1930's the point of no return had been reached. Peaceful change was the indicated formula, but by now Germany was primarily interested in "change," the Western democracies in "peaceful." [19]

The moral position became confused as condemnation of the aggressive regimes blended in Anglo-Saxon breasts with a rising sense of *mea culpa*. Searching for ways to ride with history instead of colliding with it, a few diagnosticians wrote off as historically inevitable the *anschluss* with Austria and even the absorption of Czechoslovakia. Italy's drive for a North African empire and Japan's penetration into non-

Japanese cultures were seen as calling for something more sophisticated than outright condemnation. "Change, even of territory, is not evil of itself," but in the degree of violence with which it takes place.[20]

DEFINITIONS OF PEACEFUL CHANGE

How was peaceful change actually defined? Was the emphasis purely on territorial arrangements, or did it include other changes in the status and role of political groupings? How peaceful did change have to be to qualify?

The answers, which varied considerably, are examined from two standpoints: first, the verbal definitions, and, second, the historical examples some authorities had in mind.

The Tenth International Studies Conference, held at Paris from June 28 to July 3, 1937, under the auspices of the International Institute for Intellectual Cooperation, chose for its topic the subject of peaceful change. Much of the creative thinking on this subject both in the United States and Great Britain was preparatory to, or in conjunction with the Conference.

The definition of peaceful change with which it opened was:

> . . . peaceful solution of certain international problems: the basic difficulties in, and the procedures for, the peaceful solution of economic, social and territorial problems with special reference to questions of population, migration and colonization, and markets and the distribution of raw materials.[21]

The general rapporteur of the Conference, in presenting this rather broad definition, said: "If war is to be eliminated, it is indispensable to provide other means of satisfying the profound need for change of which war is the expression and the instrument." Changes in the *status quo*, he continued a trifle opaquely, are "only those changes which derive from their international legal character certain minimum guarantees." [22] Proceeding from the broad premise laid down in the definition, the conference organized itself into a variety of subdivisions: demography, raw materials, markets, colonial questions, national and ethnical questions, and questions regarding the Danubian region.

The London School of Economics organized a symposium in preparation for the International Studies Conference, and the first lecture was entitled "What is the Problem of Peaceful Change? " Rather than defining peaceful change, its purposes were examined. People seek peaceful change procedures because (a) they wish to avoid war, (b) they wish to produce justice, and (c) they wish to produce a world order better adapted to contemporary processes and attitudes. But the kind of change represented by transfer of territory is rarely done peacefully.[23]

Arnold Toynbee, whose contribution followed, was more definite: peaceful change first of all has to do with sovereignty over territory. As to the requisite degree of peacefulness, his definition was: "peaceful *and* voluntary change." [24]

Across the ocean, likewise preparing for the Paris Conference, Professor Frederick S. Dunn took much the same line:

> The term "peaceful change" . . . refers simply to the alteration of the status quo by peaceful international procedures rather than by force. The "status quo" is the existing distribution of rights and possessions as established or recognized by the legal system. In the international field, this means primarily territorial distribution, since, through the operation of the concept of sovereignty, dominion over territory carries with it practically all other things which nations desire to possess.[25]

He went on to explain that the *status quo* also includes any situation established by treaty or by international law, including such limitations on state action as the Rhineland regime. "Any peaceful procedure for altering either the existing territorial distribution or the status of any nation would be regarded as a procedure of peaceful change."

"Peaceful change," he concluded, "is concerned both with changes in the distribution of rights and possessions and changes in the laws which govern the acquisition of rights and possessions."[26]

Others also emphasized territorial problems:

> Pending the full realization of federalism . . . orderly procedures for adjusting territorial disputes must be available. This, of course, is of the essence of "peaceful change," for it affects the *legal* rights and interests of states.[27]

Another British definition of peaceful change was: "political changes dealing with transfer of sovereignty or an alteration of the existing status of a state or area." This approach was deliberately limited to relations among "civilized powers," and excluded "imperialist" changes, as well as "purely" economic ones.[28]

Dulles listed the following categories of change in his more catholic definition: changes affecting the moral and social standing of a nation and its nationals; changes in a nation's international political and economic influence; and changes in national territory (which he readily admitted were the thorniest variety).[29]

Still another study considered the effects of peaceful change:

> . . . a regularized process for effectuating modifications in law and policy of the economic and political relationships between nations, which will be so satisfactory to the dissentient elements that the threat of wars breaking out through their aggression may be removed, but which will not be so distasteful to the defenders of things as they are that these will not make their agreement contingent upon the outcome of a trial by battle.[30]

Finally, and inevitably, was the purely legal definition. Peaceful change is "the acceptance by States of a legal duty to acquiesce in changes in the law decreed by a competent international organ." This is the only proper meaning of peaceful change as an effective international legal institution.

As a process, it can take place by denunciation of treaties, mediation, or negotiation. But the problem

> . . . is not how to induce States by moral persuasion or by appeal to political expediency to give up existing rights . . . [It is] what are the regular constitutional means of effecting peaceful change without the consent of the State which sits tight on its rights? This can be done only by overriding legislation.[31]

In the same mood a Belgian jurist wrote a few years later: "Peaceful change validates dynamism only in so far as it can be harmonized with lawfulness." [32]

But an American jurist, writing in 1943, saw signs of approaching maturity in "the conviction that change can be neither ignored nor prevented and that the world belongs to those who manifest the capacity to direct it . . . War today is essentially international revolution. It is a revolt against some part of the international order which has become intolerable to a nation or to a group of nations." [33] This view, drawing on analogies to be found in municipal law,[34] saw the key to law and order in "the existence, supported by a consensus, of an adequate organization and procedure for controlling and directing change." War will be eventually eliminated "not by the strategy of prevention, but by the development of an adequate procedure for controlling and directing change in international relations." [35]

A good deal of attention was paid to the question of the scope and degree of peacefulness involved in peaceful change. In one opinion, peaceful change did not include settlements which were the direct result of wars, and there was little disagreement with this. The results of bloodless wars were excluded as well.[36] Others took the position that any change was peaceful if it took place without actual bloodshed.[37]

HISTORICAL EXAMPLES OF PEACEFUL CHANGE

A number of participants in this debate, looking back through history, drew illustratively on the concrete changes in legal status and external relationships that various nations and territories had undergone.

There was general agreement that the most characteristic manifestation of political change — the transfer or transformation of territorial sovereignty — had rarely been accomplished peacefully.[38] When change did take place without war, there was invariably a contingent threat of war. The *ultima ratio* of force furnished an indispensable background for the evolutions that had taken place in modern times in the map of Europe.

The usual mode of transferring territory during the nineteenth century was outright cession with a suitable *quid pro quo*. Where the sovereignty of an area was in legitimate dispute — that is, not simply coveted — the cause was often inadequate drafting of geographic boundary lines, or the absence of precise expression in the pertinent treaty.

While after 1815 peaceful exchange of territory became a rarity, no boundary dispute or question of contested jurisdiction by itself led to European war in the period. The methods of resolving territorial disputes ranged from simple treaties of cession, to agreements that the parties would abide by the findings of boundary commissions. The preferred American method was outright purchase, but in Europe sales or cession of territory were often made contingent on the results of a plebiscite.

Various exemplars of peaceful change, as seen by the historians of the 1930's, are listed in the Appendix to this Chapter. The categories used are the ones suggested by those historians[39] although other examples have been added. The purpose of including this material is to demonstrate more concretely just what was in the minds of those who, in their intense preoccupation with peaceful change, turned out to be thinking almost exclusively of territorial readjustments in nineteenth- and early twentieth-century Europe.

Two traditional types of peaceful territorial change are

notable by their absence. One kind that antedated the modern period was traditionally achieved by royal marriages. In the face of such dynastic wars in the first half of the eighteenth century as the Spanish, Polish, and Austrian Successions, the Hapsburgs' foreign policy probably deserved the accolade it had earlier received: *Bella gerant alii; tu, felix Austria, nube*! However, despite the best efforts of the Bourbons and Bonapartes, by the third decade of the twentieth century as a useful means of peaceful change this was thoroughly passé.

Likewise the vast unexplored and unclaimed, or still legitimately disputed areas of the world — the *res nullius* of an earlier era of imperialism — were rapidly vanishing in the nineteenth century, and this type of change was also minimized as a source of instructive examples.

Practically all the examples given were territorial in nature. But one analysis included economic concessions made by one state to another, such as the Cobden Treaty of 1860, the Franco-Italian Commercial Treaty of 1899, the economic provisions of the General Act of the 1884 Berlin Conference, the Open Door policy in China, and the Anglo-German agreement of 1914 to share the construction of the Berlin-Baghdad railway. It also embraced such agreements as the granting of permission to immigrate and emigrate between countries.[40]

Two areas of change that were still less precise were peaceful penetration, which usually meant the special position of the powers in China (and perhaps ought also to have included the opening up of Japan); and changes in relative strength, for which two examples were the Chinese elimination of Manchu hegemony by the technique of absorption, and fluctuations in great power status such as the loss of that status by Sweden (forcefully), by the Netherlands (peacefully), and by the Ottoman Empire (by remaining inert in a moving world).

Peaceful penetration is highly pertinent to contemporary

problems of peaceful change, but in the 1930's few connections were made between peaceful change and totalitarian techniques of penetration of boundaries through ideological, political, economic, cultural, and other nonmilitary means.[41]

As for the large number of examples that were given, it is possible to draw some conclusions, but only by abandoning the subject categories their authors employed, such as Modification of Treaties, Peaceful Separation, and others, and setting up new categories that refer, not to any particular method or result, but to the factors that enabled the change to take place peacefully. If this is done, four new headings emerge which help to illuminate the political setting in which peaceful changes have on occasion taken place in the past.

(1) The first group consists of changes that stand out as having been comparatively easy to accomplish. Among the parties there already existed a strong common bond, whether racial homogeneity, similarity of culture or social structure, or a common geographical patrimony. Such evolutions as the development of the British Commonwealth, or the peaceful separation of Norway from Sweden partake of one or all of these qualities. So do some of the chapters of American continental expansion, and indeed the confederation and subsequent union of the colonies would have been a first-rate illustration. (It would also have illuminated the features that differentiate it from a world federation that is often projected by analogy.[42])

(2) In another group, peaceful change was possible because of the indifference, the weakness, or the sense of guilt on the part of the great powers, as with Germany's gradual repudiation of the provisions of the Versailles Treaty.

(3) A third group consists of unilateral acts of peaceful change stemming from motives that were ideological or economic or idealistic, more than they were strategical. The preliminary steps in the United States' grant of freedom to the Philippines should have been cited. The Soviet Russian

grant of independence to Finland, the independence of India, the repeal of the Platt Amendment, and the termination of the League mandates in Iraq and Syria, were evolutions that were made possible by the strength of political ideologies functioning in conjunction with the forces of nationalism, self-determination, and increasingly articulate mass opinion.

(4) By far the largest and most significant group involved acts of peaceful change that took place because one or another great power, concerned with its own strategic national interests, used its power and influence to bring about the change. Examples were the independence of Greece, the British-Turkish trade over Cyprus, the American and British pressure on Japan to relinquish the Shantung Peninsula, the British-endorsed breakaway of Belgium from the Netherlands, the multipartite agreements redistributing the residues of the Ottoman Empire, the great power arrangements for a regime in the Black Sea and the Straits, the independence and guaranteed neutrality of Luxembourg, the transfer of Nice and Savoy to France, and one might add the peaceful aspects of the withdrawal of European hegemony in Latin America and the Caribbean.

The choice of method or procedure was not particularly significant in the absence of this sort of motivation analysis (although it seems significant that peaceful change by means of judicial or quasi-judicial process was distinguished by its absence). For example, there is nothing to show that "peaceful separations" are in general any more promising or more frequent than "modification of treaties by consent," or that "diplomatic negotiations" will necessarily continue to include more examples than "international legislation" (although the latter rarely takes place without the former, and international legislation in the case of the League's endorsement of the termination of the Iraqi mandate, was *post factum* ratification rather than genuine legislation).

The category of purchases can probably be excluded as a

useful or important method of peaceful change, just as the previous analyses excluded dynastic marriages. Multilateral action of one sort or another — without necessarily committing the solecism of styling it all international legislation — may become a more potent force for change in the future than any previous category. But Arnold Toynbee's evaluation can still stand for the period in which it was written:

> On the whole . . . the salient fact about the peaceful transfer, or even the peaceful exchange, of territorial sovereignty in the past has been the extreme rarity of any such international transactions . . . it is probably true to say that hitherto even the most morally advanced human communities have, with very few exceptions, only reconciled themselves to parting with territory when they have been forced into parting with it by some decisive defeat in war.[43]

PRESCRIPTIONS FOR ACTION

What solutions followed from the diagnoses of the problem of peaceful change that were made in the 1930's? What light, if any, appeared at the end of the tunnel?

There was unanimous agreement on the need for peaceful change in the world order, whatever shape that order assumed. No responsible voice, outside of France, suggested that the *status* should remain absolutely *quo*, or that change was not sometimes desirable, or that the forces pressing against the established order were anything but horrendously real. And there was general agreement that, although other factors entered the equation, the question of territorial status was paramount.

But the prescriptions were as various as the diagnoses, usually tending to reflect the political orientation of their sponsors. Broadly speaking there were two general categories. There is a certain temptation to call the first the realistic-pessimistic school, and the second the idealistic-moralistic-legalistic-utopian. But these two sets of labels, so convenient as pigeonholes in which certain contemporary publicists are prone to file the rest of us, do not fit the situation with any real precision (in addition to making value judgments that often seem unwarranted).

However, for convenience the first group can be labeled realistic, in that it was innately pessimistic about the capacity of legal incantations and moral exhortations by themselves to transform the processes of politics and history. It recommended a posture of flexibility and ability to adapt in the face of events. It felt keenly a sense of the onrushing of history, whether conceived as a dialectical process, or as the *continuum* that Bergson and the metaphysical philosophers called a "state of flux." In this view, change was inevitable, stability a purely temporary phenomenon built on a base of shifting sands, and, in the words of Tennyson's couplet, "our little systems have their day, they have their day and cease to be." This group deeply believed that "War does not always arise from mere wickedness or folly. It sometimes arises from mere growth and movement. Humanity will not stand still." [44]

Edward Hallett Carr in 1939 wiped the slate clean. International law, organization, legislation, or morality could not by themselves or in combination be thought to possess the capacity to master the political process. Perhaps unconsciously reflecting the dilemmas (and mistakes) of British policy in the thirties, he went on to say:

> Any international moral order must rest on some hegemony of power. But this . . . like the supremacy of a ruling class within the state, is in itself a challenge to those who do not share it; and it must, if it is to survive, contain an element of give-and-take, of self-sacrifice on the part of those who have, which will render it tolerable to the other members of the world community. It is through this process of give-and-take, of willingness not to insist on all the prerogatives of power, that morality finds its surest foothold in international . . . politics . . . The process of give-and-take must apply to challenges to the existing order. Those who profit most by that order can in the long

run only hope to maintain it by making sufficient concessions to make it tolerable to those who profit by it least.

He recommended a foreign policy that oscillates between "force and appeasement." [45]

Following closely behind, John Foster Dulles, rejecting any identification of the doctrine of *pacta sunt servanda* with the real-life maintenance of law and order, observed that in any case change usually prevails over a static order. Man cannot prevent change so his object should be to deflect its impact away from important values which it might put in jeopardy, even if the material assets cannot be salvaged. The timing of counteraction is absolutely crucial, since these situations are malleable for only a brief time. The mechanism of change thus must have four salient characteristics: (1) it must be able to detect at the outset the stirring of forces operating for international change; (2) it must appraise accurately their growth potential; (3) it must estimate the likelihood of their finding adequate outlets through the existence or creation of internal opportunities; and (4) it must be able to recommend promptly such alteration of the international status as seems desirable and necessary in the premises.[46]

In the same vein Professor Toynbee deprecated the ability of international mechanisms to reproduce those inner qualities which permitted the British Empire, for example, to evolve peacefully into the Commonwealth. He concluded:

> If peaceful change is to become the rule, if, that is, it is to occur not simply as an *ad hoc* expedient for staving off some great war or revolution, you must have some regular method for the perpetual redistribution of power, of wealth, of population, and of the goods of this world as well. I am afraid one sees no precedents for this in the history of the past.[47]

There was a suppressed corollary to these intensely political diagnoses. On the one hand, they seemed to say, there is very little likelihood that any international agency in a world of sovereign states can hope to handle successfully the redistribution of the world's shares and the redressing of its profound imbalances. Collaterally, one is encouraged to assume that the power to do what needs to be done to keep the world society from perpetual violence is essentially a legislative power, not a judicial one. Why? Because any legal order is by definition inapplicable to the political process of change, and also because the juridical approach to these problems in a legal world characterized by self-help and self-judgment had been discredited. What effectively neutralized our own American state boundaries, for example, was the vesting in a central government of the hitherto decentralized powers over immigration, interstate movement of goods, and the coining and control of money.[48]

So the "realistic" view saw only two alternatives in speaking of peaceful change, or indeed, of world peace itself: the alternatives of all or nothing. The world would continue to blunder into wars because no machinery that candidly reflected the present level of law and social organization was adequate to manage imaginatively and successfully the vital processes of change and adjustment. The inescapable corollary of this was that an enforceable legislative process *would* be able to do what is necessary. If the latter was rejected, there remained no middle ground. Some "realists" flirted with the legislative solution,[49] but none embraced it consistently.

By *not* rejecting the supranational solution, the other school of thought believed it saw the way out. Professor (now Judge) Hersh Lauterpacht spoke most decisively for this outlook. The very existence of Article 19 of the League Covenant, he wrote, "has tended to obscure the need for the only true solution, namely, a legally binding and effective machinery of peaceful change through international legislation." This meant what it seemed to mean: a world state. The international legislature must deal not only with territorial problems but with migration, tariffs, and raw materials.

Weighted voting would be necessary because it would be utopian to expect unanimity in such a body. Of course such legislative powers would need to be backed with sanctions (and incidentally might by themselves therefore lead to war).

What was the alternative? "If an international legislature is impossible and unacceptable, then peaceful change as an institution is impossible and unacceptable." [50]

But an American opinion urged that nations concentrate on the "task of equipping international society to direct change, rather than an adventure in the impracticable strategy of prevention." In this view the sanctions system under Article 16 of the League Covenant was "premature, impracticable, and should be eliminated," since there were no collateral techniques for facilitating change.[51]

Another popular solution took the form of an equity tribunal (which played a certain part in the pre-Covenant planning, and again today occupies considerable favor in private Charter revision planning). One planner envisaged such a tribunal as a part of the Permanent Court of International Justice.[52] In another view, if the equity tribunal's proposals went unheeded, the League Assembly should impose the solution by a qualified majority vote, including all the major states not parties to the dispute. Still others recommended that such a "law" of peaceful territorial change in time be extended to economic and colonial relationships.[53]

But the majority of suggestions lay somewhere between the two extreme positions. For example, it was considered idle to devise procedures for peaceful change "unless these procedures frankly embody the notion of coercion," but the legislative solution was usually dismissed with the comment that it was also a waste of time to devise procedures and institutions of peaceful change "which would work if only nations were more rational or less nationalistic." Since under present conditions "the only demands for changes in the status quo which receive the serious consideration of the international community are those which involve a threat of disturbance of the peace if not satisfied," the answer was a relatively modest formula:

> . . . procedures adapted to persuasion, investigation, the discovery of compromises, the revealing of real interests and objectives, the determination of the general welfare, the organization of opposition, the marshalling of public opinion, the manipulation of pressures and means of coercion short of actual resort to hostilities.[54]

Another set of findings, based on an exhaustive study of the history of warfare, recommended a changed human outlook:

> This investigation . . . has convinced the writer that the problem of preventing war is . . . essentially one of maintaining adaptive stability within the world community, only possible if larger sections of the public . . . view that community as a whole.[55]

Others prescribed "a will to permit change and machinery to provide adjustments."[56] Some suggested greater use of the plebiscite technique;[57] others urged greater use of mediators.[58]

The Paris Study Conference, referred to earlier, ended its deliberations in a mood of pensive uncertainty of which it is hard to be critical even today. Its conclusions centered around the need for more effective international organization, but with a strong conviction of the importance of the intangible sources of motivation behind demands for changes in the *status quo*, and behind the often irrational opposition such claims encounter. The delegates departed still unable to decide whether the world was ready for a regime armed with imperative methods and compulsory judgments.[59]

It was inevitable that intimate connections be made between the notions of peaceful change and collective security. The latter dominated Geneva in the 1930's, and for good reason. A typical view pinned all the blame on the policeman:

> In the international field in the course of the last twenty years,

the legislator has been active but has lacked boldness, and the judge has been conscientious but has lacked authority. The policeman, on the other hand, has been neither active nor conscientious and has lacked boldness and authority.[60]

If the problem had been stated in terms of security, and not exclusively collective security, it might have made better sense. This was done in yet another presentation, taking security as a sense of confidence. Discarding the alternatives of a supranational state, an international equity tribunal, an international police force, or greater national altruism, it was suggested that three other avenues be explored: (1) tackling each problem separately instead of as part of an overwhelming and unmanageable force, and attempting to get reasonable compromise solutions; (2) calling for a general conference looking toward a negotiated "package" settlement; and (3) reinvigorating the peace system of the League. But at the end it was necessary to settle for a sort of moral rearmament of the *status quo* powers to prepare themselves to face up to the problem of peaceful change, and to take the actions necessary to ensure that justice was done.[61]

Another approach was that the role of collective security was to prevent changes which the community did not sanction from taking place:

. . . no system for peaceful territorial change appears to be possible until states are assured that collective security is so reliable that only claims which are based on justice as interpreted by international bodies can ever be successfully promoted.[62]

And a somewhat unusual point of view on the peaceful change-force equation was this:

Under the Covenant, in the event of a nation having gone through (the Article 15) procedure and having got no redress it was entitled to go to war unless the other side accepted the report of the Council . . . the framers of the Covenant felt that, without that kind of pressure, you would never get any alteration of the *status quo*. You either had to put behind Article 19 the coercive powers which are now behind Article 16, or you had to allow the individual nation to bring these coercive powers to bear. What has happened since is that the hatred of war has grown and has been stimulated by the Kellogg Pact, and resort to war has become the central crime. That is not the Covenant at all. I have always thought that the strength of the Covenant in its original form was that it did permit some pressure whereby changes could be made.[63]

There was a certain degree of dogmatism in statements about this relationship:

> Forceful holding against peaceful revision is ethically as bad as conquest, perhaps, but not as dangerous to either peace or orderly progress as is violent effort at revision; collective security is less of an obstacle to peaceful change than is persistent effort at violent revision . . .

So far so good. But,

> Whoever and whatever obstructs collective security obstructs peaceful change whether by unanimous agreement or by majority vote.[64]

It is no longer necessary to agree with this unqualifiedly. Legal force ultimately proved to be at the service of states that defended the established order. There was at no time during that period any evidence that such force would be equally at the service of those who would alter the *status quo*.

In retrospect, the real alternatives were either to acquiesce in changes in the *status quo* (as with the Munich Agreement), or to resist changes with force (as with World War II). There was never the alternative of somehow forcibly enforcing the changes, although it was this supposition that lent symmetry to many theoretical statements on the subject of peaceful change. The real relation between peaceful change and collective security continued to rest on a most uncertain base.

THE DEBATE IN PERSPECTIVE

It is difficult to sum up this debate. In 1938 one might have concluded that there existed an urgent need to rethink the premises of international law in order that the political *status quo* not be confounded in every particular with legal right. A reexamination seemed indicated of the holdings of the Western democracies, with a view to sharing some of their bounty with the Axis powers. According to this argument, Chamberlain's conveyance of Czechoslovakia at Munich, while undoubtedly the wrong deal at the wrong place, was on the right track. Appeasement was still a respectable word, and was founded on a viewpoint that had its own interior logic.[65]

From the vantage point of today such a summation is grossly incomplete. It is now clear that by 1938, only total surrender would have appeased Hitler, whose ambition turned out to be not equilibrium but empire. The arguments of the 1930's lacked the insight that the impulse behind Hitler was messianic, not rational, ideological, not economic, nihilistic, not negotiable.

There was a catastrophic time lag in the West between the sowing of the seeds and the reaping of the harvest. The voices raised in the 1930's were, in truth, speaking to the problem of 1919, not 1939. "The owl of Minerva begins its flight when dusk is falling." By the time creative thought intervened, only a policy of forceful opposition could have deflected the events then in train. With a few notable exceptions, such a policy was unthinkable to a generation imbued with the ideology of pacifism, rationalism, and the postulated harmony of interests in the postulated community of nations.

The revolution was taking shape, backed by increasingly uncontrollable force. By the middle of the 1930's it could have been stopped only the way internal revolution is classically halted — by treating it as an intolerable revolt against the established order. By calling it that, yet not so treating it, the dominant majority paralyzed itself not only politically but morally as well.

There are parallels between this period and the present one. But one sovereign difference in the quality of intellectual perception is thrown into sharp relief with the incomparable advantage of hindsight.

There seemed little comprehension of the fundamental differences between the value systems represented by the *status quo* and anti-*status quo* powers, a comprehension powerful enough to link those differences to the problem of peaceful change. The image furnished by the historians of that era is one either of unappeasable military juggernauts in motion, or of a set of rational economic and geopolitical pressures that could be assuaged by shrewd and timely action to relax the grip of the satisfied powers on marginal resources and territories.

But one seeks in vain for what so many of them liked to call a "facing up" to what had in their day become the overriding source of international tension and conflict — the fundamental incompatibility of the two types of social organizations, democratic and fascist. The present age must be highly sympathetic to the passionate desire to find alternatives to war, which after all was not very different from what today goes under the heading of the search for peaceful coexistence. Yet today's tragic dilemma is at once heightened and made more intelligible through the recognition of the single matrix in which the contemporary conflict of values coexists at each and every point with the problem of stability and change.

Appendix: Some Historical Illustrations of Peaceful Change

Definition of an ultimatum: The last warning before resorting to concessions. — Ambrose Bierce

INTERNAL PEACEFUL CHANGE

The transformation of the British Empire into the British Commonwealth, seen as a *de facto* process of which the 1931 Statute of Westminster was simply the formal ratification.

MODIFICATION OF TREATIES BY CONSENT

The abolition of capitulations in Turkey in 1914, with indirect British agreement, thus ending the regime of consular courts which had been established by the so-called capitulation treaties.

The Japanese renunciation of the former German holdings on China's Shantung Peninsula, as well as of Weihaiwei. This was embodied in the Sino-Japanese agreement of 1922, following the application of great pressure by Britain and the United States. (It is technically true that Japan did not sign the Versailles Treaty, which this example was intended to illustrate, but Japan's position in Shantung was stipulated in that treaty.)

The modifications of the Versailles Treaty so far as reparations were concerned, through the Wadsworth Agreement (1923), the Paris Agreement (1925), The Dawes Plan (1925), the Young Plan (1929), and the German-American Debt Agreement of 1930. (In 1932, of course, the Germans unilaterally repudiated their residual obligations.[1])

PEACEFUL SEPARATION OF TERRITORY

The formation of modern Greece was often cited. While Greek separation from the Ottoman Empire was the outcome of the Greek War of Independence from 1821–1831, the later accretions of the Epirus, the Ionian Islands, Thessaly, and Crete were generally without violence, usually under British sponsorship.

The breakup of Czarist Russia was presented as a mixed example, Georgia's unsuccessful attempt to secede having been met by the Bolsheviks with violence, Rumania's occupation of Bessarabia accepted as a *fait accompli*, and positive consent given to the ultimate independence of Finland.

The secession of Norway from Sweden in 1905–6, ratified by the Treaty of Carlstad, was a prime example.

The creation of the Irish Free State, with British consent, in 1921. (Actually, what was granted was dominion status, and this act followed on a virtual state of revolution lasting many years.)

The independence of Belgium (1830) was at least ratified by collective community action, in that the powers, under British lead, declared the dissolution of the Kingdom of the Netherlands following the Belgian revolution.

PEACEFUL UNIONS

The union of Scotland with England, initially with the personal union resulting from the accession of James I in 1603, and leading to wars and insurrections (such as the Second Civil War), but culminating in the peaceful and lasting union of 1707.

That phase of the Italian *risorgimento* when in 1860 the provinces of Tuscany and Romagna, plus the Duchy of Parma and Modena, through peaceful plebiscites, voted to annex themselves to Piedmont.

The somewhat similar phase of German unification, culminating in the voluntary agreements in 1871 between Bismarck and the rulers of the South German states, with Bavaria the only reluctant joiner, enlarging the North German Confederation to become the German Empire.

The Government of India Act of 1935, setting up provisions for the peaceable accession of the native states to an All-India Federation. (This led to such later unpeaceful acts of adherence to the new India as that of Hyderabad, but other princely states entered the union peacefully.)

CHANGES IN TERRITORIAL RELATIONS, WITH TRANSFERS OF SOVEREIGNTY

Again, the evolution of the British Commonwealth was cited.

The 1878 *de facto* British occupation of Cyprus, in a horse-trade with Turkey also involving French and Italian penetration into Tunisia and Albania, respectively (the latter was abortive), confirmed by British annexation in 1914.

The Anglo-German agreement of 1890 by which Germany relinquished large claims in East Africa in exchange for Heligoland, which Britain had acquired from Denmark in 1815.

Often, the favorite example was the Austro-Hungarian acquisition of the provinces of Bosnia and Herzegovina by mandate of the powers at the Congress of Berlin, 1878 (followed in 1908 by Austrian annexation of the provinces).

A related act was the creation of the new states of Montenegro, Serbia, and Rumania by the Berlin Congress of 1878, actually ratifying the Treaty of San Stefano between Russia and Turkey.

CHANGES BY THE JUDICIAL PROCESS, THE PARTIES AGREEING IN ADVANCE

The Bering Sea Arbitration between the United States and Great Britain in 1893 and,

The North Atlantic Coast Fisheries Arbitration between the same countries in 1910, were generally cited as classic illustrations of how sovereignty questions affecting marginal waters could be resolved by the judicial or arbitral process.

The Free Zones of Upper Savoy and the District of Gex were the objects of a judgment by the Permanent Court of International Justice, the significance of which was that France and Switzerland, dissatisfied with the judgment, empowered an arbitral tribunal, in effect, to legislate a regime for the region in question.

EXTINCTION OF SOVEREIGNTY

Under the Act of the Congress of Vienna, Geneva, which had been independent until annexed by France in 1798, lost its independence *de jure* through inclusion in the new and independent confederation of Switzerland, but gained certain special rights in the process.

NEW INTERNATIONAL STATUS WITHOUT CHANGE IN SOVEREIGNTY

The perpetual neutrality of the Swiss Confederation guaranteed by Act of the Congress of Vienna (1815).

The acquisition by Belgium of both independence and neutrality in the years 1830–1839 (backed strongly by Britain as an extension of the Barrier Policy aimed at France).

There might have been added a category of peaceful territorial changes resulting from the principle of compensations in the distribution of colonial territories. Also, two sphere-of-influence divisions of territory were: Ethiopia in the treaty of 1906 between France, Britain, and Italy which followed the traditional Polish pattern; and the 1907 agreement on Iran between Britain and Russia. Neither case involved outright cession, but portions of the territory were reserved for the exclusive benefit of one power.

Three types of territorial change which some historians accepted but which a few ruled out of bounds or at least put at the far limits of peaceful change, plus a fourth category that seems equally plausible, are:

UNILATERIAL DENUNCIATION OF A TREATY WITHOUT NEGOTIATION

In 1870, capitalizing on the Franco-Prussian War, Russia denounced the clauses of the 1856 Treaty of Paris neutralizing the Black Sea.

The 1908 Austrian annexation of Bosnia and Herzegovina (which was cited by still others as a peaceful change of sovereignty, without attaching undue significance to the stigma of treaty repudiation).

The 1936 German remilitarization of the Rhineland, in violation of the Treaty of Versailles.

PEACEFUL CHANGE ACCOMPANIED BY THREATS OF WAR

The Franco-Prussian agreement by which the independence and neutrality of Luxembourg were guaranteed by the powers in the 1867 Treaty of London (possible only because both Napoleon III and Bismarck preferred a sounder *casus belli*).

The settlements between Great Britain and the United States on the joint boundary north of Oregon and Maine (which were peaceful settlements only because large-scale war never actually broke out and time had healed the chronic irritations of the years previous).

CHANGES MADE IN PREPARATION FOR WAR

The agreement between Napoleon III and Count Cavour of Piedmont at Plombières in 1858, ceding Nice and Savoy to France as part of the program of provoking Austria into war.

CHANGE IN STATUS, BUT ONE STEP REMOVED FROM WAR

Even if direct results of war are rightly excluded from examples of peaceful change, still, assuming that the acquisition of mandatory status by the former German colonies actually followed an intermediate stage when they were either the outright spoils of the victors of 1919, or were *res nullius* as a result of the termination of German control,[2] it might be argued that the second-stage change to mandatory status was bloodless and peaceful.

One other approach reviewed the history of peaceful change from the businesslike standpoint of the diplomatic processes by which peaceful changes were accomplished, settling on four principal functional categories: change achieved by diplomatic negotiation, by conciliation, by international conferences of the bargaining variety, and by international legislation.[3]

DIPLOMATIC NEGOTIATIONS

Louisiana Purchase from France, 1803.

Gadsden Purchase from Mexico, 1853.

Purchase of Alaska from Russia, 1867.

United Kingdom cession of Heligoland, 1890.

British withdrawal from Samoan condominium.

Norwegian secession from Sweden, 1905.

Soviet-Japanese Treaty, 1924, by which Japan evacuated North Sakhalin in exchange for concessions.

United States purchase of Virgin Islands from Denmark.

Egypt's progressive change to more independent status with regard to Great Britain.

CHANGES IN THE STATUS QUO NOT INVOLVING TRANSFER OF TERRITORIAL SOVEREIGNTY

Hay-Pauncefote Treaty of 1901 by which Britain renounced its claim to a voice in the Panama Canal.

United States-Cuban treaty of 1934 abolishing the Platt Amendment.

CONCILIATION

Japan's renunciation of Shantung, 1922.

Mediation by Beneš as President of the League Council in securing Anglo-Persian agreement to new oil concession terms after Persian cancellation of the former agreement.

INTERNATIONAL BARGAINING CONFERENCES

Britain's renunciation of its 1815 protectorate over the Ionian Islands in 1864, accepted by a conference of the signatories.

Neutralization of Luxembourg by London Conference (1867).

1878 Congress of Berlin which prevented war in the Near East by revising the Treaty of San Stefano.

Recognition by the Berlin Conference 1884–5 of the Congo Free State, and agreement on general principles for trade and colonial enterprise in equatorial Africa.

1923 Statute internationalizing Tangier.

1923 Lausanne Treaty and 1936 Montreux Convention on the status of the Straits regime.

1932 Lausanne Conference abolishing the reparations clause of the Versailles Treaty.

INTERNATIONAL LEGISLATION

Termination of the mandatory status of Iraq by unanimous vote of the League Assembly, 1932.

PEACEFUL CHANGE

AND THE UNITED NATIONS

For, after all, the United Nations is only a mirror of the world political situation. —

Sir Gladwyn Jebb

The United Nations has been weak and limited in its progress . . . because [it] is still much more a mirror of the world than an effective instrument for changing it. —

Gen. Carlos P. Romulo

Chapter 6

Peaceful Change in the United Nations Charter

Article 14: Subject to the provisions of Article 12, the General Assembly may recommend measures for the peaceful adjustment of any situation, regardless of origin, which it deems likely to impair the general welfare or friendly relations among nations, including situations resulting from a violation of the provisions of the present Charter setting forth the Purposes and Principles of the United Nations.—

United Nations Charter

United States foreign policy during the 1930's had much to commend it, such as the new dignity imparted to Latin American relations. But with respect to the mounting crisis in Europe and the Far East, American policy was ambiguous and uncertain. The American people, preoccupied with domestic recovery and still disillusioned about their last sortie into the power politics of Europe, remained of two minds about where their interests lay and what their responsibilities were toward those interests.

In this atmosphere, detached verbal pronouncements often substituted for a more pointed and vigorous diplomacy. Secretary of State Cordell Hull in 1937 outlined what he conceived to be the principles governing American international relations. He communicated this document to all the other governments of the world, and they, failing to detect either a price tag or any concrete details that might be embarrassing, unanimously accepted Mr. Hull's principles.

Included in this catalogue of the great clichés and the great principles of international law and morality was this statement:

> Upholding the principle of the sanctity of treaties, we believe in modification of provisions of treaties, when need therefor arises, by orderly processes carried out in a spirit of mutual helpfulness and accommodation.[1]

After making allowances for the vagueness and loftiness of a state paper embodying general principles, this was a good summing-up of contemporary Anglo-Saxon opinion on peaceful change. It left the issue nicely balanced between the legal doctrines of *pacta sunt servanda* and *clausula rebus sic stantibus*. Read in the context of the isolationist spirit that still paralyzed the United States, and of the inability of President Roosevelt to move anywhere but backward after his Quarantine speech in Chicago three months later, it reflected accurately the quandary of the times.

It was Adolf Hitler and his partners, rather than any American leader, however eloquent, who brought about the transformation in American opinion. In August 1941, President Roosevelt and Prime Minister Churchill signed the Atlantic Charter aboard the cruiser *Augusta* off Newfoundland. After asserting that the two countries sought no aggrandizement, "territorial or other," the Charter stated, in Point Two:

> . . . they desire to see no territorial changes that do not accord with the freely expressed wishes of the peoples concerned.

And Point Four read:

> . . . they will endeavor, with due respect for their existing obligations, to further the enjoyment by all states, great or small, victor or vanquished, of access, on equal terms, to the trade and to the raw materials of the world which are needed for their economic prosperity.[2]

The second point was a restatement of the Wilsonian principle of self-determination. The fourth point was an elaboration of one of the Fourteen Points. The need was thus acknowledged for peaceful change in conjunction with the self-determination principle. With the concept of "equality of access," policy had now assimilated the idiom of the inter-war period. And here, as before, a peace settlement was promised that would be generous, not Carthaginian.

UNITED STATES PREPARATIONS

The provisions of the United Nations Charter were so much a product of the thoughts and labors of American official personnel working in Washington during the war (except for certain crucial provisions on voting and representation which had to be decided by the heads of governments, and various refinements applied at the Dumbarton Oaks Conversations and the San Francisco Conference), that a short legislative history of Article 14 can be developed in the first instance through an examination of the preparatory work done by the United States government.[3]

The revision of treaties was actively considered at the outset of discussions within the United States government. In January 1943, it was proposed that either of the parties to a bilateral treaty or two-thirds of the parties to a multilateral treaty might request a Permanent International Equity Tribunal for an advisory opinion as to:

> . . . whether the treaty or engagement, or any provision thereof, should be revised in the interests of good relations between the parties.

If there was no agreement, the proposed Council, on its own, or on motion of one of the parties, could, by a two-thirds vote, "advise the parties as to the revision which it considers to be necessary in the interests of justice and the maintenance of good relations."

As a final stage in this process of treaty revision, the doctrine of *rebus sic stantibus* was spelled out in empowering the proposed Court as follows:

> Any executory treaty or engagement entered into with reference to a state of facts the continued existence of which was envisaged by the parties as a determining factor in the acceptance of the obligation stipulated may, upon the petition of any party, be pronounced by the Permanent Court of International Justice to have ceased to be binding when the state of facts has been essentially changed.

But after a brief discussion this whole notion was rejected on the grounds that treaty revision was not essentially a juridical question, and that it would stir up dissension all over the world.

The issue arose again in the spring of 1943, in the internal discussions of a so-called Staff Charter prepared for the Informal Agenda Group and the Political Subcommittee, under Secretary Hull's chairmanship.

> The giving of authority to the Council to review treaties was considered but rejected because the Covenant article had proved ineffective. On the other hand it was considered politically impossible to go beyond the Covenant model by giving the Council the power to compel states to revise treaties or adjust conditions. However, it was hoped that the Council's power on its own initiative to take up disputes affecting peace or good understanding of nations would contribute to the attainment of peaceful change.

The first draft charter to see the light of day was entitled *Draft Constitution of International Organization*, dated July 14, 1943. It was prepared by the Special Subcommittee on International Organization within the Department of State under the chairmanship of Under Secretary Sumner Welles. It made no reference to peaceful change in the sense of revision of treaties or territorial adjustments (although Article 9, entitled "Peaceful Adjustment," empowered nations to bring to the organization conditions disturbing the peace or "the good understanding between nations," in the style of Article 11, paragraph 2, of the League of Nations Covenant).[4]

The next draft charter to be recorded in the official annals was one prepared by the staff of the Division of Political Affairs, dated August 14, 1943. This too was devoid of any such provisions, although again the question of revision of treaties had been discussed.

In a plan submitted to President Roosevelt by Secretary Hull on December 29, 1943, one of five purposes of the proposed postwar organization was "to facilitate the adjustment of conditions likely to impair the security or undermine the general welfare of the peace-loving nations." It also contained the first reference to a new function for the proposed Assembly: not only to interpret international law, but to revise it as well.[5]

On June 15, 1944, President Roosevelt issued a public statement spelling out the program for the development of what was styled a "Possible Plan" for international organization. There was no mention of any aspect of the problem of peaceful change,[6] but the draft of the "Possible Plan," as it was used in consultations with members of Congress, contained two references to the dynamics of the world order which would be represented by the proposed organization. One was the revision of rules of international law, mentioned above. The other was:

> to make, on its own initiative or on request of a member state, reports on and recommendations for the peaceful adjustment of any situation or controversy the continuation of which it deems likely to impair the general welfare.[7]

Recalling the official interpretations of Article 19 of the League Covenant which suggested that war had to be positively imminent before action might be taken, the "general welfare" clause in these drafts represented a step forward.

The *Tentative United States Proposals for a General In-*

ternational Organization, with which this government entered the Dumbarton Oaks Conversations in August 1944, contained a provision identical to this last,[8] and in essence this was what, after a certain amount of travail, became Article 14 of the Charter. (The Proposals also contained the provision on revision of rules of international law, which did not fare so well.)

During the Dumbarton Oaks talks a curious thing happened. Taking advantage of the bipartisan truce regarding this project that had been negotiated between Mr. Dulles, representing Governor Dewey, and Secretary Hull, representing Mr. Roosevelt, Governor Dewey, after examining the United States proposals, called Secretary Hull on September 6, 1944, to suggest that the text did not clearly show whether a condition, situation, or controversy arising from treaty provisions could legally be brought before any of the organs of the proposed organization. This posed the issue concretely.

But the Department of State decided that the necessary latitude was implicit in the broad scope of the language, and the British were apparently in agreement on this point. "Furthermore," Harley Notter's official record says at this point, "enumeration was generally opposed on the ground that it would call for inclusion of all possible factors, or else risk interpretation as excluding factors not mentioned. Therefore, no express references to treaties was thought necessary." [9]

The Dumbarton Oaks Proposals, representing the agreed view of the American, British, Russian, and, in a separate subsequent meeting, Chinese governments, contained the original provision in a rather terser form, in Chapter V on the General Assembly, under Section B on Functions and Powers. Paragraph 6 read:

> The General Assembly should initiate studies and make recommendations for the purpose of promoting international coopera-

tion in the political, economic and social fields and of adjusting situations likely to impair the general welfare.[10]

Senator Arthur H. Vandenberg had been a central figure in the pre-Dumbarton consultations, although he had not attended the Conversations themselves, which were limited to diplomatic officials. He had been more concerned than perhaps any other leading American figure with the possibility that the proposed organization might become committed to sustaining the *de facto* world order without regard to justice. That order would necessarily embrace the new Soviet position resulting from Russian wartime drives westward.

Vandenberg's large Polish-American constituencies in Michigan, plus his innate sensitivity to the need for accommodation in the dynamic process of politics, conspired to make him the consistent champion of flexibility in the new organization, and the opponent of any arrangements which would freeze the *status quo*, or deprive the states aggrieved by the terms of a peace settlement from subsequently seeking justice in the form of treaty revision. On November 24, 1944, he made the following entry in his diary:

> I was greatly pleased . . . My chief complaint . . . has been that we . . . through the League guarantee the ultimate status quo in the postwar world even though the status quo shall prove to be wholly unjust (as seems clearly threatened by a new dismemberment of Poland). I have been constantly told by students of the Agreement that these peacetable decisions would not be within the jurisdiction of the new League. I put the question squarely to Stettinius and Pasvolsky . . . today. After much discussion, they finally answered (to my amazement) that if any State is aggrieved as a result of the peace decisions, and it causes friction and unrest which might lead to trouble, the new League *can* take jurisdiction.[11]

Vandenberg followed up his advantage vigorously. He acknowledged that the new organization was not itself to make the peace, but insisted that its peace-keeping functions should not be rigidly wedded to an unacceptable *status quo*.

In a letter to the publisher of the *Polish Daily News* in Detroit on March 7, 1945, he wrote:

> Would it not be better to go along with the New League and make every effort at San Francisco to write the objectives of the Atlantic Charter into its dedications and seek to give it specific authority to examine at any time whatever injustice may have been inherited from the war era and to recommend correction? [12]

When the American delegation met for pre-conference briefings in Washington, Vandenberg presented eight amendments to the Dumbarton Oaks Proposals, "in behalf of 'justice,' " [13] and intended to assure that the organization should not attempt to "freeze the status quo" but would have the power to recommend adjustments whenever it found any unjust situation threatening the peace.[14]

To Chapter VIII of the Proposals on the Security Council, he suggested adding:

> If the Security Council finds that any situation which it shall investigate involves injustice to peoples concerned it shall recommend appropriate measures of adjustment which may include revision of treaties and of prior international decisions.[15]

And to the Assembly, on which attention was subsequently to be focused in this regard rather than the Security Council, he recommended empowerment to establish justice,

> . . . foster the observance of human rights and fundamental freedoms; encourage the development of rules of international law; and recommend measures for the peaceful adjustment of situations likely to violate the principles of the United Nations as declared by them on January 1, 1942.[16]

The delegation accepted this, commenting that it represented a significantly different approach than that being taken by the United Kingdom which thought of the United Nations in terms of keeping the peace in times of crisis. Eight days later, Secretary Stettinius reported to the President the alterations in the Dumbarton Oaks Proposals that had been unanimously agreed upon by the American delegation. Under Purposes, the delegation had recommended:

Inclusion of a statement that the organization should act in accordance with the principles of justice and equity in adjusting or settling disputes . . .

To the General Assembly, the delegation wished to:

Extend power to recommend measures for peaceful adjustment to include situations likely to violate the principles enunciated in the Atlantic Charter and situations arising out of any treaties or international engagements.[17]

THE SAN FRANCISCO CONFERENCE

The San Francisco Conference began on April 25, 1945, and on May 2 the United States delegation met to discuss Article V, B, paragraph 6, particularly the empowerment of the Assembly to recommend measures "to establish justice," as agreed to by the delegation in Washington. Did justice refer to justice within states, or between states, or both?

There was no decision as to its meaning, but it was agreed that it was desirable and should be retained, if only to bargain with. (At the same meeting the delegation decided to oppose, as going too far, a Brazilian proposal empowering the Court to decide if any executory treaty had lost its binding force because of changed conditions or because it had become unfairly burdensome.)

As a result of its preliminary discussion, the delegation circulated on May 2 a paper entitled *Changes in Dumbarton Oaks Proposals as Suggested by the United States Delegation.* It contained the following altered version of Article V, B (6) (marked * to show changes):

The General Assembly should initiate studies, and make recommendations for the purpose of promoting international coopera-

* In the following quoted passages, angle brackets ⟨ ⟩ indicate words stricken out; italics represent words added.

tion in political, economic, ⟨and⟩ social *and cultural* fields, *and in measures to establish justice; fostering the observance of human rights and fundamental freedoms; and encouraging the development of rules of international law.* ⟨and of adjusting⟩ *The General Assembly should recommend measures for the peaceful adjustment of* situations likely to impair the general welfare *or to violate the principles accepted by them in the Preamble of the Declaration by United Nations of January 1, 1942, including situations arising out of any treaties or international engagements.*[18]

To reconcile their separate afterthoughts regarding the proposals, the four sponsoring powers set up three subcommittees, one on the subject of treaties. The basic issue was whether the General Assembly should be enabled to consider international "situations arising out of any treaties or international engagements." [19]

The Soviet Union, always alert for the *arrière-pensée*, quite correctly took this as a pointed threat to the postwar integrity of its wartime territorial spoils. On May 4 the subcommittee met again, and this time the American draft had substituted for the phrase "arising out of any treaties or international engagements" the presumably more anodyne words "regardless of origin." [20] Agreement was reached in principle but apparently not in fact, as it was decided by the four Foreign Ministers late the same night that each government would submit separately its proposal regarding this and other unagreed matters.[21]

At midnight the same night a document was issued by the four sponsoring governments, embodying their agreed amendments. For Article V, B (6) it read only:

The General Assembly should initiate studies and make recommendations for the purpose of promoting international cooperation in political, economic, ⟨and⟩ social *and cultural* fields *to assist in the realization of human rights and basic freedoms for all, without distinction as to race, language, religion or sex and also for the encouragement of the development of international law* ⟨and of adjusting situations likely to impair the general welfare⟩.[22]

Attached as an appendix to this document was another one entitled *Additional Amendments to the Dumbarton Oaks Proposals Proposed by the United States*. Although accepting paragraph 6 as in the agreed four-power text, the United States proposed that it be followed by a new additional paragraph:

Subject to the provisions of paragraph 1 . . . the General Assembly should be empowered to recommend measures for the peaceful adjustment of any situations, regardless of origin, which it deems likely to impair the general welfare or friendly relations among nations, including situations resulting from a violation of the Purposes and Principles set forth in this Charter.[23]

By May 7 this had been agreed to by the joint sponsors; it was so issued on May 11.[24]

On May 9, Committee II/2, on General Assembly questions, debated the "regardless of origin" concept.[25] As Senator Vandenberg told the story, the committee approved "my Amendment to keep the Assembly wide open for the exploration of any subject 'regardless of origin'—thus to make it truly the town meeting of tomorrow's world, and to prevent this Organization becoming an instrument to freeze the status quo in a static world. Thus *justice* gets a forum and *injustice* loses its grip. We had quite a fight."[26]

Vandenberg was vigorously supported by the United Kingdom, and the final vote was twenty-three in favor of the sponsoring powers' amendment, three opposed, and two not voting.

In his role as United States spokesman, Vandenberg had insisted that "regardless of origin" by no means implied that the revision of treaties would be foreclosed to the Assembly as a fit subject of discussion. The Soviet Union interpreted his position as keeping a loophole open for "review and alteration of the treaties of reciprocal assistance concluded from 1942–1945 by the U.S.S.R. with Poland, Yugoslavia, Czechoslovakia, and also France as being incompatible—in his mind

—with the Charter . . . At the same time he was assuring the United States an opportunity to tailor to its taste any treaties among European powers, at will and through the use of the U.N." [27]

The Vandenberg interpretation was very much in the foreground as other delegations offered their comments and amendments to the Dumbarton Oaks Proposals and the four-power amendments.

Egypt, for example, urged that the Assembly have the right "to advise, on the request of any member concerned, the reconsideration of treaties which have become inapplicable." Mexico (unlike most of its Latin American brethren) believed that the Assembly should have the right to examine "treaties proving inapplicable and any international situations having become unjust." [28] Egypt, Brazil, and Mexico all proposed amendments designed to grant the Assembly the right to invite the parties to a treaty to undertake its revision.

But the chief emphasis in the discussions of paragraph 6 and its new sequel was on the desirability of somehow blending with it the idea of international law (as suggested by Australia and Liberia) and the concept of economic aggression (favored by Peru), and of combining the two paragraphs into one in order to link more closely the secondary causes of war with the proposed adjustment of situations.[29]

At this point the problem of treaty revision arose again in United States delegation meetings. France had proposed that observance of treaties be deemed an essential condition of international order. Senator Vandenberg pointed out that he had sought review authority for the Assembly precisely so it could alter peacefully the many dubious treaties extant. France seemed to be taking a legalistic stand in order to neutralize Vandenberg's proposal, but it was believed that the French also had some specific treaties in mind, such as the mutual assistance treaty with the Soviet Union, and treaties with Near Eastern states.

The delegation agreed finally to support the insertion of the phrase "due respect for treaties" in the Preamble. (Also, over Senator Vandenberg's objection that it would confirm Russia's war-swollen boundaries, the delegation agreed to support a New Zealand-Australian proposal that states refrain from the threat or use of force against any state's territorial independence or political integrity — which was to become Article 2, paragraph 4.)

In the American delegation meeting on May 23, however, there were a number of second thoughts on including the "respect for treaties" clause in the Preamble, as the French had proposed. While some Latin American delegations, it was pointed out, were strongly in favor, others felt it would be too rigid, even though it would not be legally binding in the Preamble.

Subcommittee II/2/A on May 17 submitted to Committee II/2 three questions regarding revision of treaties, based on amendments by Brazil, Mexico, and Egypt:

1. Should the Assembly be empowered to examine treaties which appear to be inapplicable and to make recommendations to the governments (parties thereto) and to the Security Council with respect to such treaties?

2. Should the Assembly *at the request of any member concerned* be empowered to recommend the reconsideration of treaties which have become inapplicable?

3. Should the Assembly, *at the request of any party to an executory treaty* claiming its inapplicability or the injustice of its continuation, be empowered to invite the contracting parties to agree to the revision or cancellation of the treaty? [30]

There was some delay in Committee II's response due to a problem of competing jurisdiction, but, on June 1, Committee II began discussion of these questions.

It was in this debate that the definitive American gloss was placed on the "regardless of origin" clause, to locate it, at least in the American view, in direct line of succession to Article 19 of the League of Nations Covenant.

On that same day the United States delegation had decided that the language agreed upon under the heading of "peaceful adjustment" would adequately cover the question of treaty revision, and it undertook to oppose any amendments aimed at reopening the matter of revision.

Thus, in Committee II the United States delegate explained that, although he had originally contemplated a specific allusion in the Charter to the question of revision of treaties, the broader language of paragraph 6 had now been agreed to by the Big Four. This had been done because "it was inconsistent to launch an international organization based on international integrity and at the same time to intimate any lack of respect for the instruments through which international integrity functions, namely treaties." The General Assembly's concern would be, not with treaties *qua* treaties, but "with adjusting conditions which might impair peace and good relations between nations. Considerations of the general welfare may call for a recommendation that a treaty be respected rather than revised." But, the "regardless of origin" phrase "should not be interpreted to mean that the subject of treaty revision was foreclosed to the Assembly. If treaties give rise to situations which the Assembly deemed likely to impair the general welfare or friendly relations among nations, it could make recommendations in respect of those situations." [31]

In the discussion that followed, Egypt, disclaiming concern with any specific treaty, expressed astonishment and regret that Article 19 was not reproduced in the Dumbarton Oaks Proposals, but agreed to go along if the record clearly showed that treaties were within the purview of the new article.[32]

In the meeting of Committee II two days later, the United Kingdom announced its agreement with the American exegesis. The Soviet Union, on the contrary, asserted that any provision regarding revision of treaties "would contradict the principle of the sovereignty of states . . . The task of the Conference was not to shatter the foundations of treaties and sow doubts, but to strengthen respect for treaties. It would be particularly dangerous to insert . . . a provision which would undoubtedly undermine all the systems of agreements with enemy states already concluded and of peace treaties yet to be signed." [33]

The Czechoslovak delegate, arguing with fine inaccuracy that Article 19 had been "a sort of legal cover" for Germany's prewar policies, supported the Soviet position. Peru deplored the juridically imprecise situation resulting from the United States interpretation. Ecuador suggested that the Assembly, on the application of one party, invite the other party to negotiate, and, if the parties disagreed, the International Court of Justice could decide if the treaty should be altered. France assumed the expected posture of hostility to any possibility of treaty revision.[34]

The discussion concluded the next day, marked only by the Chilean delegate's assertion that if any sort of treaty revision procedure were written in, "peace and security would be imperilled." The Committee voted, thirty-seven to one, to withdraw the three questions,[35] and Article 14 remained essentially as it had been drafted by the United States on May 4 in the Big Four Subcommittee.

Subcommittee II/2/B on June 5 considered one other change in the language of paragraph V, B (6). Some delegations, particularly China, felt that the Assembly should be empowered to initiate studies and make recommendations for promoting the revision of international law (which the United States had discussed in its earlier deliberations). The Committee voted in this sense at its tenth meeting, but three of its eight members believed that the original language which spoke of "development" of international law was adequate if the word "progressive" preceded it.[36] At the meeting of

Committee II on June 7 the more modest alternative carried by a vote of twenty-eight to eight.[37]

Thus, when Committee II ultimately presented this section to its parent body, Commission II, the language read "and also for the encouragement of the progressive development of international law and for its codification," [38] which is the language of the present Charter (Article 13, paragraph 1 (a)). Thus the principle of revision of international law was relegated, along with its big brother, the revision of treaties, to constitutional limbo.

In the debate in Commission II on the report of Committee II, several speakers addressed themselves again to the revision of treaties, the *status quo*, and peaceful change.

It is not inconceivable that they had also taken cognizance of the work of Committee I/1 on the Preamble of the Charter, which was discussed within the American delegation in terms of treaty revision. In his report to that Committee on June 5, the Rapporteur of Subcommittee I/1/A had stated:

> The respect for treaty obligations and the pledged word under any form is not only a moral concept of high value but is undoubtedly an important factor in international order and stability. Order, however, should not be conceived as the negation of healthy international evolution, nor should stability imply the crystallization or the freezing of the international *status quo*.[39]

The Rapporteur of Committee I/1, reporting to Commission I, said it only slightly differently:

> Law and stability, however, cannot be rendered distinct from justice, and stability should not be conceived as a negation of healthy international evolution.[40]

So when the French representative in Commission II asserted that there was nothing in the Charter resembling Article 19 of the Covenant because Hitler had used that artical as the basis for his territorial claims, and it was thus calculated to destroy the world's chance for "stability," the room echoed with the history of a policy that was as futile as it was consistent. The French attitude toward revision was supported, needless to say, by the Soviet Union.[41]

The Belgian delegate hastened to correct the defective French version of history. Article 19, he pointed out, had nothing to do with Nazi and Fascist aggression. The absence of a provision in the new Charter for revision of treaties was not for the reason adduced by France, but "because it appeared to us to be politically sounder not to encourage revision campaigns."

The drafters of Article 14 had succeeded in their frank intention to leave the language vague and imprecise to the point of semantic instability. The delegate of Colombia asserted without qualification that by this language the revision of treaties was absolutely excluded. Bolivia and Egypt, on the other hand, expressed confidence in the Assembly's capabilities under the proposed language to deal with revision as the "foremost" item in the catalogue of techniques for maintaining world peace.

The report was thus adopted on the basis of completely different understandings as to what the language really meant.[42]

The official American position was summarized in Secretary Stettinius' report to the President:

> The United States Delegation took the position that explicit reference to the revision of treaties would throw the weight of the Organization too heavily on the side of revision and encourage change beyond the needs of situations requiring it. It was argued that it is not possible to launch an international organization based on international integrity and at the same time intimate any lack of respect for treaties, which are the principal instruments through which international integrity functions. Indeed, a consideration of the general welfare and friendly relations might call for a recommendation that a treaty should be respected by its signatories rather than that it should be revised. The thousands of treaties in operation as the bond of orderly relations among the

nations of the world, should not be weakened by raising doubts about their value or permanence.

On the other hand, if situations exist under treaties which are alleged to impair the general welfare or to threaten friendly relations between nations, or to conflict with the purposes and the principles of the Charter, such situations shall be open to discussion or recommendation by the General Assembly.

It was the view of the United States Delegation, therefore, that the General Assembly should not interest itself in a treaty per se, but rather in the conditions and relations among nations which may impair the general welfare or friendly relations among nations. These threats to the general welfare may arise from treaties or from situations having no relation to treaties. In any case, as soon as situations emerge as a threat to the general welfare, they should become a matter of concern to the General Assembly. Thus the broad powers entrusted to the General Assembly will enable it to render effective aid in the difficult process of "peaceful change." [43]

THE RATIFICATION OF THE CHARTER

In the hearings on the Charter before the Senate Committee on Foreign Relations in the month following completion of its drafting, some further light was shed on the concept of Article 14. "The General Assembly," said Secretary of State Stettinius in his opening statement,

. . . has the further power to recommend measures for the peaceful adjustment of situations regardless of origin likely to impair the general welfare, including situations resulting from violation of the purposes and principles of the Organization. This is one of the most important provisions in the Charter for peaceful change and for the correction of injustices present or future.[44]

Coming down to details, the Committee aimed its questions at the late Leo Pasvolsky, then Special Assistant to the Secretary of State for International Organization and Security Affairs, and the American expert par excellence on the detailed provisions of the instrument. His testimony stands as the definitive United States interpretation of the significance of

Article 14 and of what happened at the San Francisco Conference to give that article its final meaning:

Mr. PASVOLSKY; Article 14 is, from the point of view of the General Assembly, the counterpart of the primary function assigned to the Security Council. The Security Council has primary responsibility for dealing with situations which relate to the maintenance of international peace and security. Article 14 gives the General Assembly the function and the power of recommending measures for the peaceful adjustment of any situation regardless of origin which it deems likely to impair the general welfare or friendly relations among nations.

The CHAIRMAN (Senator Connally): Right there, I want to say that the credit for the adoption of the phrase "regardless of origin" is due the Senator from Michigan, Mr. Vandenberg. That phrase was the subject of a good deal of discussion and debate in the committee of which the Senator was a member. "Regardless of origin" is an all-embracing phrase and opens up to the discussion in the Assembly almost any question that has arisen since Adam and Eve were in the Garden. I think it is a very wise one and a very good one.

Mr. PASVOLSKY: . . . If the situation is of such a nature that it may threaten international peace and security, then Articles 11 and 12 apply, and the General Assembly, instead of taking action itself, would have to refer the situation to the Security Council. But if a question of the maintenance of international peace and security is not involved, then the General Assembly is completely free to perform this vastly important function of helping the world to operate on the basis of stability and justice and fair dealing.

Although the contrast was not drawn by those present in the Caucus Room, Dr. Pasvolsky's explanation removed from Article 14 the disability which the 1921 Committee of Jurists had read into Article 19 of the Covenant, namely the incapacity of Article 19 to become functional except in the presence of "international conditions whose continuance might endanger the peace of the world." The new Article, Dr. Pasvolsky was saying, was designed to cope with conditions in their early stages, before they had become explosive, and before positions had hardened to the point where war or surrender were the only alternatives. If this were indeed to be the case, it was probably justifiable to assume that it would "help the world to operate on the basis of stability and justice and fair dealing."

The next exchange served as counterpoint to the last one, and showed Senator Vandenberg's continuing concern with the political aspects of peaceful change, notwithstanding the toning-down at San Francisco of his favorite theme, and the role he had since played as apologist for that process of dilution.

Senator VANDENBERG: Would it be fair to say that this article assures us against any static world?

Mr. PASVOLSKY: I think it definitely does.

The questioning then turned to the relation of Article 14 to the revision of treaties. In answer to a question from Senator Austin, Dr. Pasvolsky replied:

MR. PASVOLSKY: The phrase "regardless of origin" obviously relates to treaties or to any other conditions which may cause the sort of situation that is envisaged here.

Senator AUSTIN: Then this article undertakes to make the General Assembly a sort of court of review of such treaties as now exist; is that right? . . .

Mr. PASVOLSKY: Not a court of review of treaties, but a court of review of situations arising out of whatever conditions have been brought about, either by treaties or in other ways.

Senator AUSTIN: Does the record indicate that this power includes the power to recommend the modification of treaties?

Mr. PASVOLSKY: It states that the General Assembly may recommend measures for the peaceful adjustment of any situation. Suppose the situation arises out of a condition created by a treaty: The General Assembly would necessarily have to consider whether or not the situation arose out of a lack of performance under the treaty or out of the onerousness of the terms themselves or the applicability or nonapplicability of the terms of the treaty.

Senator AUSTIN: Then, carried to its logical conclusion, if the Assembly should decide that the terms of the treaty were onerous, and that that was the cause of the situation, the record indicates that Article 14 gives authority to recommend a modification of those onerous terms; is that right?

Mr. PASVOLSKY: Of course, that would be included among the measures for the peaceful adjustment of the situation, which the Assembly is given the right to recommend.

Senator VANDENBERG: I would like to comment on that question. When this article was originally written it specifically included reference to the revision of treaties. There was objection to the specific identification of revision of treaties lest it seem to be an invitation to take apart these international contracts, the integrity of which necessarily goes to the very roots of sound international relationships. Properly the objection was made that the reference to the revision of treaties might seem to be an invitation for the revision of the peace treaties with our enemies. Therefore, since the objective was not the revision of treaties, but the revision of conditions, this substitute language was agreed upon . . .

In other words, we said what we meant. We did not mean to put the emphasis upon the revision of treaties; we meant to put the emphasis upon the revision of conditions. Those conditions may arise out of any source, regardless of origin. They may arise out of the failure to enforce a treaty. They may arise out of the onerous conditions of a treaty. There may be . . . other reasons besides the revision of treaties which are responsible for these conditions which impair the general welfare. The revision of treaties is not identified, because when it was identified it seemed to be the sole objective of the article . . .

Given the likelihood that the original United States formulation was jettisoned at San Francisco because of fierce Soviet opposition (much as it had been at Paris in 1919 by French opposition), Senator Vandenberg's explanation put the best possible face on it. Indeed, it made sense, given his newly refurbished premises. But his keen awareness of the present was no longer matched with as keen an awareness of the past. It was already forgotten that the justification for revisionary clauses in both the Covenant and the Charter was the need, demonstrated over and over again in history, to palliate the discontent of those who were on the losing side in wars and to whose disadvantage the territorial settlements were always drawn at the peace table.

There were, moreover, two new factors. The World War II territorial settlement was even then in the process of being made unilaterally by the Soviet Union. And the Soviet Union itself was rapidly becoming the new "enemy." This may not have occurred to all the 1945 debaters, but it had occurred to Mr. Vandenberg time and again before the San Francisco Conference. So "an invitation for the revision of the peace treaties with our enemies" had a new meaning, and not necessarily one detrimental to United States interests.

Still, in July 1945, the United States was dealing with the old set of enemies, a multilateral peace settlement was confidently envisaged, and few could foresee the vastly different stage setting to come when the curtain dropped on this act and rang up for the next one.

A few more questions completed the hearings on Article 14. Senator Connally drew on his fund of picturesque imagery to wrap up the analysis of the "regardless of origin" phrase:

The CHAIRMAN: And the origin of (a situation) is immaterial. The question is its existence, no matter whether it crawled out of a cave or came down from the heavens. It is a question of whether or not the situation exists, regardless of what caused it . . .

Senator VANDENBERG: May I add that when it includes situations resulting from a violation of the provisions of the present Charter setting forth the purposes and principles of the

United Nations, it includes the principle of equal rights and self-determination.

Senator AUSTIN: One further question. Is it true that there is no sanction involved in the execution of Article 14, and that its validity and vitality rest upon the self-discipline of the nations involved?

Mr. PASVOLSKY: I think so; I think that is right. There is no sanction there except a moral sanction . . .

Senator AUSTIN: It is true, is it not, that throughout this document there is a conscious effort to stimulate self-discipline of nations in order to prevent war?

Mr. PASVOLSKY: Most assuredly. That is one of the basic considerations here.

Senator VANDENBERG: It is the paramount consideration.[45]

CRITIQUE

Throughout the period of planning, the overriding consideration was security. That security was to be achieved by internationalizing the responsibility of suppressing German, Italian, and Japanese militarism. The urgency of that job completely overshadowed the tentative gropings for a formula for peaceful change. There was an uneasy awareness of the need to plan on the basis of a dynamic rather than a static world. A certain amount of lip service was paid to this feeling, and verbal solutions, progressively more vapid, were embraced.

But so overwhelming was the feeling of "never again," so demanding the call for machinery to underwrite that feeling, and so absorbing the impulse to systematize the world order in the image of the wartime coalition, that the founders, along with practically all their contemporaries, lacked the perspective to see the ephemeral nature of the political order they were seeking to establish. And of course the modalities of diplomacy precluded candid discussion of the Soviet Union's intentions regarding Eastern Europe, Egypt's determination to repudiate its treaty agreements with Great Britain, France's fears of German recovery, or Senator Vandenberg's wish to be able to tell his constituents that Poland would be liberated through, if not by, the United Nations. Such candor was not a legitimate expectation of the diplomatic process.

Article 14 was, like Article 19 of the League Covenant, a compromise. It eliminated mention of treaty revision but provided instead for General Assembly consideration of problems affecting the general welfare which would, at least in the American view, include demands for changes in treaties, boundaries, or the *status quo* in general.

History can be critical of the San Francisco Conference for forgetting, in the excitement of the moment, the poignant history of the League, the complex meaning of the *status quo*, and the ramifications of peaceful change. But however the draftsmen had behaved, and whatever words went into Article 14, the application of this "peaceful change" article had to depend on the political situation at the time it was invoked. This was true of the League and it has been consistently true under the United Nations. As it worked out, the drafters of Article 14 neither helped nor hindered the process of peaceful change.

There was a curious irony in the planning on peaceful change and on security. In assigning the "peaceful change" function to the General Assembly, what the planners had in mind was a species of democratic action, rather than great power rule. On the other hand, the security provisions of Chapter VII were premised on great power, not democratic action. Neither has worked out quite the way it was planned. The new meaning of collective security has had to be supplied by the political realities of the times. Similarly, the capabilities of the United Nations for peaceful change, and the import of those capabilities for the United States, must be read in terms of how they have worked out in practice.

The act of creation was only the backdrop against which the drama has been played out.

Given the temper and the political imperatives of those times, only a bold man could claim that under the circumstances he would have acted differently. And yet, one is tempted to agree with a wise student of affairs that:

> Perhaps one of the reasons why so little is learnt from experience is that the men who conduct the affairs of nations are always changing, and that too few of them read history. This is particularly true of democracies.[46]

The delegates at San Francisco had available to them the same rearward vision that men have today with respect to 1945. In the attempt to impose on the unruly residue of international politics a regime that would restructure the war-torn world, notions of how that world ought to function were written into the Charter, and some others written out, for reasons which did not always stem from a rational evaluation of the situation and a sense of historical realities.

There might not have been better solutions. But there might have been better understanding of the perpetual warfare between the *status quo* and the energetic movements, for good or evil, that it breeds. If the language of Article 14 had not been changed by so much as a semi-colon, a sense that such understanding existed would still be a mild comfort if one suspects, with Santayana, that "Those who cannot remember the past are condemned to repeat it."

Chapter 7

The Past: 1945 to 1957

Men wiser and more learned than I have discerned in History a plot, a rhythm, a predetermined pattern. These harmonies are concealed from me. I can see only one emergency following upon another as wave follows upon wave. —

H. A. L. Fisher, *A History of Europe*

The United Nations has functioned in a rapidly changing world. At times it has been at the center of the storm, and at other times has seemed isolated from events. But at all times it has faithfully mirrored the political turbulences of its age. Even when external forces have appeared in only symbolic form in the organization's debates and resolutions, important meanings could be read into those parliamentary expressions. For the exterior struggles have assumed concrete shape in the development of voting blocs, in the trading of one set of goals against another, and in the coalescence of symbolic power in the votes that have taken place on crucial issues before the General Assembly.

Two of the forces that have found their way into the air-conditioned chambers alongside the East River have accounted for the deepest tensions in the modern world. These are the force of world communism which acquired sufficient material power in World War II to extend its reign through Eastern Europe from the Baltic to the Adriatic and, with communism's victory in China, to the Sea of Japan; and the force of nationalism in the former and present colonial areas of the world, bred by World War II to politically decisive proportions.

THE EAST-WEST CONFLICT

When the East-West conflict made its early and dismaying appearance in the United Nations, one would have thought the stage set for a classic struggle between the *status quo* and revolution, an antithesis dogmatically formulated by Karl Marx in these words:

> Impotence . . . expresses itself in a single proposition: the maintenance of the *status quo*. This general conviction that a state of things resulting from hazard and circumstances must be obstinately maintained is a proof of bankruptcy, a confession by the leading Powers of their complete incapacity to further the cause of progress and civilization.[1]

The Soviet Union was still a dynamically expanding power, dedicated to revolution in the non-communist regions of the world. But Russia had at the same time won a military victory of tremendous proportions, that had moved its sphere of control from the Dnieper to the Elbe, and whose fruits it had no intention of relinquishing.

So in terms of the territorial *status quo* in Eastern Europe, paradox became policy, and Soviet Russia became in this sense a new force for conservatism. Wartime pledges to help the liberated countries "create democratic institutions of their own choice," and to underwrite "the restoration of sovereign rights and self-government to those peoples who have been forcibly deprived of them," [2] ran directly counter to Russia's new power position and were cynically repudiated.

Meanwhile the program of social revolution was still carried on with ruthless persistence by the successors to the Third International, employing all the classical tactics in the revolutionary arsenal, ranging from clandestine subversion to overt infiltration into labor, parliamentary, and other mass parties of the bourgeois states.[3]

But the dialectic proved, as usual, flexible enough to encompass the expansion of Russian military power and political hegemony. Moscow installed subservient governments in the Soviet orbit which, except for Yugoslavia, were for a decade rigidly controlled. To reinforce this control with the appearance of legality, a network of treaty relationships was established, most recently the mutual security treaties redundantly linking up the monolithic communist empire in a parody of the North Atlantic Treaty Organization.

The Western powers, having withdrawn their forces from the continent except for occupation troops, looked on helplessly while the new empire set its watches along the borders of Central Europe. Once again, as twenty-five years before, they were nagged by a sense of responsibility for what had happened. In addition, this time their leaders, particularly in the United States, faced a public opinion that would never understand such failure of policy. And with the final triumph in 1949 of the communist revolution in China, they were tormented by the nightmare of Mackinder's "world-island" as a grotesque reality instead of a hypothetical theorem of geopolitics.[4]

Thus, it was the United States and its Western allies who were profoundly discontented with the *de facto* territorial dispositions, who agitated against them, whose policy toward the captive peoples was formulated in terms of liberation from their new masters, and who were only too glad to have in the United Nations General Assembly an international forum in which these grievances might be kept alive.

With the death of Stalin and the spread of Titoism through much of the satellite orbit, new forces of liberalism seemed to be penetrating the barriers of dictatorial rule. The revolts in Poland and Hungary, no matter how ruthlessly suppressed, have given a new dimension to the problem. But the basic confrontation of forces in Eastern Europe, and the attitudes of the Western powers toward them, remain unchanged, albeit acutely sharpened.

THE NORTH-SOUTH CONFLICT

So far as the colonial world was concerned, nothing would ever be the same again. Since World War II, one quarter of the world's population had broken away from Western colonial rule. In the war the Western rulers had been ejected from Southeast Asia and supplanted by Asians, ending forever the myth of white invincibility. In other regions such as the Middle East and Africa the virus of freedom and national self-determination became epidemic as it spread by word and image from its spiritual home in the West to areas never seriously contemplated for its propagation.

The new nations were weak in material power, but they had a spirit our own nation can recall if it looks back a hundred and eighty years. They were bound to the remaining colonies by ties of consanguinity, a common heritage of grievances, and religion — a force that Henry Adams once said could be used in politics like gunpowder.[5] Spiritually and numerically strong but materially weak, they found in the General Assembly of the United Nations an ideal forum of expression. There the Yemen commanded the same voting strength as Great Britain; the Philippines was equal to its liberator, the United States; Syria was on a par with its former mandatory, France.

There were other programs in the United Nations that dealt with these problems. Under the trusteeship system eleven trust territories were established [6] (though all but Somaliland were former League mandates). With a total population of a little under 18,000,000, and covering approximately 907,000 square miles, they fall under the purview of Article 76 which defines the basic objective of the trusteeship system as, among other things, the promotion of "progressive development towards self-government or independence as may be appropriate to the particular circumstances of each territory and its peoples." Thus, Chapter XII of the Charter may be considered the first of the organization's battery of cyclotrons, so to speak, committed to accelerating the pace of change from dependent to independent status.

In addition, between sixty and eighty other non-self-governing entities have at one time or another in the past ten years been reported on to the United Nations by administering powers that were bound by Chapter XI. The population of the non-self-governing territories is around 150,000,000, and their total area 6,500,000 square miles—twice the size of the United States.[7]

The United Nations is not the only active agency in this picture. The British freed India, Burma, and Ceylon with no reference to the United Nations. Some administering states, often working with dedication to bring a dependency to a position where cutting the umbilical cord would not mean its immediate suicide, have determined for themselves that a territory has become self-governing. Thus, frequently the issue is one of the tempo of developments rather than the principles. But the United Nations was created with constitutional responsibilities which often are depicted as substitutes for the authority of the responsible states. The Charter itself requires members to "recognize the principle that the interests of the inhabitants of these territories are paramount, and accept as a sacred trust the obligation to promote to the utmost . . . the well-being of the inhabitants" and, above all, "to develop self-government." Above all, that is, in terms of the emphasis that the anti-colonial world has placed on Article 73 as the second potential constitutional stimulant to action toward freeing the remaining colonies from Western rule.

These two sets of currents, running between the poles of East and West, and North and South, have created a political rip tide which directly affects United States interests. For example, our ability to muster satisfactory majorities on crucial cold war issues has become increasingly dependent on the position we take with respect to unrelated colonial issues. In the Assembly the anti-colonial forces are able to swamp the votes of the administering states with votes of states that do not have the responsibility, unlike the Trusteeship Council where the two forces are in parliamentary balance. The anti-colonial coalition includes a growing number of stragglers from the Latin American bloc, which normally votes with the United States.

The Arab-Asian grouping, with help from these increments of strength including the votes of the Soviet bloc, reached a climactic point in the vote in October 1955, to inscribe the Algerian question on the Assembly's agenda. That a formula was subsequently found whereby the inscription vote was left unimplemented and France enabled to resume her seat with some grace, only serves to illustrate the flexibility of the forces in whose favor the tide has now turned.

ARTICLE 14 IN PRACTICE

Both the cold war and the colonial issues have been modified to a certain extent in their impact within the United Nations by the constitutional limitations of the organization. The Soviet-Western confrontation has been affected, if not estopped, by Article 107 reserving the unilateral rights of the powers with respect to the ex-enemy states. And the anti-colonial revolution has had to take into account the provisions of Article 2, paragraph 7, which forbids the organization to intervene in "matters which are essentially within the domestic jurisdiction of any state." In both cases the lines have been crossed and recrossed where there existed sufficient political incentive. The record of interpretations placed on Article 14 in debates tends to confirm the predominance of political interest over issues of intrinsic legality.

A review of those interpretations over the past ten years produces few surprises.[8] The primary constitutional issue raised under Article 14 was the competence of the Assembly to make recommendations in given cases. Article 10 was usually employed in conjunction with 14 to ensure its applicability to a broad range of issues, while Articles 107 and 2(7) were the principal legal weapons of defense.

Article 107 was invoked, usually by the communist bloc in East-West cases, as inhibiting the competence of the organization. Article 2(7) was invoked, usually by the colonial powers, to restrict the Assembly from intervening in such cases as French North Africa and the racial situation in the Union of South Africa (not a peaceful change case but one resting on Article 14's general provisions). The communists have, however, opposed General Assembly action with respect to Hungary on Article 2(7) grounds.

The other constitutional issue involved the measures the Assembly could take to implement Article 14. In the original Palestine case this arose most acutely, since the partition plan was not acceptable to one party — the Arabs — and while the Assembly could only recommend, the partition scheme was widely interpreted as a species of legislative action requiring enforcement.

The United States generally interpreted Article 14 liberally, particularly in East-West cases such as German elections, but with difficulty in some of the colonial cases in which this country was subject to strong pressures from its Western European allies.

The Soviet Union, on the contrary, saw Article 107 as forbidding United Nations discussion of the Korean problem, but in the earlier Palestine case and particularly on colonial issues, has favored a broad interpretation of Article 14, as opposed to Article 2(7).

The ancestral issue — revision of treaties of peace — arose only once, in an abortive Argentine proposal that the Italian Treaty be revised.[9]

The history of interpretations of Article 14 does not tell

the full story of peaceful change under the United Nations. For one thing, peaceful change issues have arisen in organs other than the Assembly, the Security Council, for example. They have sometimes been problems of pacific settlement of disputes, sometimes problems of trusteeship or non-self-governing territories. The Charter has proven a flexible instrument, and frequently action has been taken with no reference at all to specific Charter provisions. Change is a process that will not halt for constitutional or parliamentary reasons. If a problem of changing relationships is evaded at one juncture, it tends to return at another point, or in another fashion.

The actual issues of peaceful change in the United Nations can be examined without having to worry very much about whether they referred to Article 14, or some other article, or no article at all.

TWENTY-TWO CASES

Out of the thousands of items that have appeared on the agendas of the various organs of the United Nations in the past ten years and on which action [10] of one sort or another has been taken, twenty-two stand out as being related to the process of peaceful change as we have defined it. They have not by any means all resulted in peaceful change. Some, while successful as change, have not been peaceful. Others are still under consideration. But they all genuinely relate to the transition, successful or unsuccessful, of a territory from one political and legal status to another, primarily by means other than overt military warfare.

Seventeen peaceful change issues were debated by the Assembly: Spain, SouthWest Africa, Palestine, Korea, Indonesia, Jerusalem, Italian colonies, Morocco, Germany, Tunisia, Togoland, Austria, Cyprus, West New Guinea (Irian), Algeria, and, most recently, Suez and Hungary. Six — Indonesia, Spain, Palestine, Korea, Hungary, and Suez — were at one time also on the agenda of the Security Council. Five more — Kashmir, Trieste, the Sudan, Hyderabad, and Formosa — were separate Security Council cases.

There may be argument about the inclusion of some of these. In the first group, the Spanish question is included with misgivings, although the few writers who have looked into peaceful change in the United Nations (and whose listings are far narrower than the one here), have usually cited it. Boiled down to its essentials, it was a matter of trying to alter the form of government in Spain, but is included to demonstrate that internal peaceful change is a separate and special problem, usually unsuitable for multilateral action.

The Hungarian case has been anything but peaceful; nonetheless, the Assembly has voted to call for steps which, if taken, would perforce alter Hungary's political status with respect to the Soviet Union, presumably by peaceful means.

Jerusalem is listed separately because, while it was debated under the broad cloak of "the Palestine question," the very attempt to transform that city into a *corpus separatum* argues for its separate listing.

As for Hyderabad, while action was never taken by the Security Council, it is included as one of the few problems of peaceful change (or the lack thereof) involving Asiatic peoples exclusively. It is useful to know that occasionally it is the Eastern rather than the Western ox that is gored.

(Another comparable example is worth mentioning parenthetically. This was the abortive revolt against the new state of Indonesia by the islanders of Ambon in the South Moluccas, who set up a Republic of the South Moluccas in April 1950, and were suppressed by force of Indonesian arms in November 1950, while Indonesia drew around itself the cloak of domestic jurisdiction it has since been engaged in stripping off the Western democracies. The Security Council was invited by the United States to discuss the Ambonese question but there were no takers, and meanwhile the insurrection had been at least temporarily suppressed.[11])

It might be useful to list these cases in terms of the conflict patterns that give the political world its contemporary shape, both inside and outside the United Nations. (The details of the individual cases are either well-known or are amply dealt with elsewhere.[12])

In the first category would be the East-West cases involving peaceful change: Trieste, Korea, the Austrian Treaty, the Italian Colonies (which are also included under another heading), the problem of free elections in Germany, Formosa, and Hungary. (Hungary is an obvious example of failure.)

The second category deals with colonial relationships, where the issue is primarily between the colony and its metropole: Morocco, Tunisia, and Algeria; Indonesia; and Hyderabad (not precisely a colony but probably not a state either, and included in this category for convenience). Cyprus has a secondary place on this list.

The third category also contains colonial cases, but those where the issue is primarily among states (usually including the metropole), rather than chiefly *vis-à-vis* the dependency itself: SouthWest Africa, Palestine, Jerusalem, the Sudan, Cyprus, and West New Guinea.

Fourth are the colonial territorial cases where no major international dispute existed: the Italian colonies again, and Togoland unification.

Fifth are non-colonial territorial issues of peaceful change between states in the free world: Kashmir and the international status of the Suez Canal.

Sixth is the inevitable category of miscellaneous: Spain.

GENERIC ISSUES

In addition to those cases, three other topics in the United Nations have had what might be called a generic bearing on the process of peaceful territorial change. These issues of principle, so to speak, are Self-Determination, Administrative Unions, and the Transmission of Information on Non-Self-

Governing Territories (including the cessation of such transmission). All are in the colonial field and at least bear on the transfer of territorial sovereignty from one legal *locus* to another. And they reflect the three-cornered relationship the anti-colonial forces wish to see strengthened between the administering power, the dependent territory, and the organization, acting, not in the form of expert opinion and guidance to the mandatory powers, as the League did, but by majority votes of representative of states.

The appeal of self-determination is tremendous, whatever verbal modifications surround and hedge it. It evokes the shades of the American Revolution, Woodrow Wilson, and the whole pattern of colonialism a United Nations majority seems determined to exterminate. As such, it can be taken as a potent symbol of the direction the organization is now taking, and a central feature of the process of change, whether peaceful or bloody.

As for administrative unions, the Trusteeship Council set up a standing committee in 1950 to ensure that the operation of such unions "does not have the effect of extinguishing the identity and separate status of trust territories." [13] The case of SouthWest Africa is a concrete example of this problem.

Information from non-self-governing territories involves the question of factors to consider in determining when there has been a change in status, and it also involves cessation of reporting from the administering authorities. In November 1954, the following paragraph was adopted by the Assembly by a vote of thirty-three to twelve, with five abstentions (the subject was the termination of reporting on Greenland by Denmark):

> Bearing in mind the competence of the General Assembly to decide whether a Non-Self-Governing Territory has or has not attained a full measure of self-government as referred to in Chapter XI of the Charter.[14]

The United States, maneuvering in an ever narrower space

between the two contending groupings, voted against this paragraph. But it bespoke the power of the anti-colonial faction to pass "rules" as to where authority rests for decisions about the change of colonial territories to a new status.[15]

THE JUDICIAL PROCESS: A FOOTNOTE

Of the thirteen-odd contentious cases so far brought to the International Court of Justice, only one could be described as a problem of peaceful territorial change. This was the question of whether France or Britain had sovereignty over the miniscule Channel Islands of Minquiers and Ecrehos. The Court unanimously decided, on November 17, 1953, that the United Kingdom was the rightful owner,[16] and it is fair to say that they all lived happily ever after.

CONCLUSIONS FROM THE RECORD

Great caution is called for in drawing conclusions from the cases listed above. Any patterns or trends that may have been revealed were based on a relatively small amount of evidence over a relatively brief historical period.

Still, some things can legitimately be inferred, while reserving for future judgment their universal applicability, or even the prediction that they may be repeated in similar ways in seemingly identical cases.

The first finding is that, as with the League, the involvement of the great powers was an important factor in determining whether peaceful change would come about, and how. If behind the facts of a case was the direct clash of interests between hostile great powers, as in Korea, Germany, Austria, and Formosa, United Nations action was either impossible or greatly limited. Only time will demonstrate this proposition with respect to the Hungarian case. If only one side was in a position to intervene, however, such transitions as those in the former Italian colonies and the political change regarding South Korea were possible, although not always through the United Nations, as in Trieste.

Second, even where the great powers were not directly involved, the ability of the United Nations to advance solutions to their conclusion often depended on the order of magnitude of the problem to the parties. It has not been in the interests of the Western powers, for various reasons, to press the Assembly's reiterated recommendations to the Union of South Africa to place SouthWest Africa under trusteeship. Nor has the Indonesian-Dutch dispute over West New Guinea stirred them to a decisive posture one way or the other.

A third variable was the degree of intensity of feeling generated by an issue, that is, whether, as in the Court's award on Ecrehos and Minquiers no one really cared, or, as in both the earlier and current aspects of the Palestine case, everyone cared deeply. It is no accident that the one was adjudicated, the other dealt with by political and military procedures rather than by arbitration or judicial settlement. The factor of intensity is real enough to suggest reexamination of the assertions by proponents of legal methods that the intangibles of such cases are irrelevant or, at best, easily avoidable.

Fourth, without a doubt the very fact of United Nations involvement in a case can affect the development and outcome, on the ground as well as in the organization. It can be argued that United Nations debate incites to riot by encouraging the extreme claims of dissidents. But it can also be argued that things would be worse, not better, if allowed to find their own political level unaided by the United Nations. The question is hypothetical, and only history can judge if the effect is primarily to pacify difficult situations by providing a safety valve, or whether, as some colonial powers claim, the organization's interference is the decisive factor in worsening local situations.[17] It is difficult to believe that a negotiated solution regarding Suez could have done the damage on all sides that resulted from unilateral attempts at solution.

Indochina can be compared with Indonesia to support the conclusion that, all things being equal, United Nations action (in Indonesia, for example) can result in a more stable international position than the extremely untidy procedure followed by France in Indochina.

This in turn suggests that, as in Indonesia, Palestine, and Korea, the most significant role of the United Nations was to endow with international legitimacy the political arrangements arrived at by political and diplomatic processes. In this sense, the legal function of the United Nations is of major importance, but is not to be confused with a legal order in terms of which political decisions are made. On the contrary, the legality the organization can supply with its procedures and facilities (including the *imprimatur* of election to membership, as in the case of Austria, Libya, Tunisia, and Morocco) follows, rather than precedes, the acceptance of a political conclusion. Legality in the United Nations is not the cause of political acceptability, but rather its consequence.

This leads inevitably to the question of whether the United Nations is properly capable in the peaceful change field of what is loosely called "international legislation," meaning recommendatory action that is interpreted to represent the insistent will of the community which should, if necessary, be enforced as though it were legally binding. In the Palestine case, the practical justification for United Nations action was that the organization actually had little real choice in the matter. The British were going to liquidate their increasingly sanguinary commitment and, as in the case of Greece the same year, someone had to pick up the pieces. If no responsibility had been assumed by the United Nations for a solution, it still would have had to take responsibility under Chapter VI and possibly Chapter VII.

When the United Nations becomes seized of situations of

this order, common sense suggests that it must undertake to find longer-range solutions even while coping with the short-run effects. Having done this, the United Nations must take its lumps for exercizing a function that it could not see through when one of the parties balked, and which perpetually arises to plague it in the relations between the Arab States and Israel.

These problems present themselves all too frequently, and must be dealt with somehow. In some instances, as with Kashmir, only time can moderate the position of the parties, and meanwhile the fuse has been withdrawn from the powder keg. In Indonesia and Palestine, the explosion had started, and action was insistently demanded by the facts.

Where great power harmony existed, or where there was prior agreement among the parties, or where there was at least a determination to proceed along pacific lines, success has attended the United Nations' participation in the peaceful change process. The Italian colonies case satisfied the first criterion; the Court's disposition of Minquiers and Ecrehos, the second; and the end of the trusteeship for British Togoland, the third. It may be that peaceful change is impossible unless one of these three factors is present. Of course, the situation can become so inflamed, as in the Near East, that determined efforts will be made to press the sort of pacific settlement efforts that can break through to the new ground of peaceful change.

There is a curious semantic in the political and legal phase of the anti-colonial revolution. Such cases as Hyderabad, Cyprus, West New Guinea, and the abortive South Moluccan revolt, tended to show that special interpretations are being placed on commonly understood concepts, much as the Marxists have consistently done in their own field of political warfare.

Is a matter internal when the peoples in conflict are racially homogeneous, and international when they are not? Is a matter international when blue water separates two areas, and internal when they are contiguous? Is the determining factor the involvement or the concern of third parties, without which there would be no real international dispute?

The first two criteria cannot be found anywhere in the law, but seem to represent the real-life working of the principle of self-determination in the present age.[18] The third, in the colonial field, is an operational factor that helps bring the "law" to bear where the matter might not otherwise become litigated. There is a certain temptation to meet hypocrisy squarely wherever it is encountered. In the colonial area it might be theoretically possible to relax the pressures of the Arab states on the European powers, or of the Asian states on the Union of South Africa, by passing resolutions condemning slavery in the Arabian peninsula and the residues of the caste system in India, advising on Christian-Moslem relations in Lebanon, and arranging for international disposition of the outlying districts of Indonesia which that government still has not brought under control.

But the argument, like the argument in the 1930's, is not always a rational one. It is more practical to evaluate with as much historical detachment as possible the revolutions in process, and to consider first of all the true interests of the participants and the other nations in solutions aiming toward peace and stability in the area, and in the world. The inter-Asiatic cases do imply that rules of thumb about peaceful change — indeed, about politics generally — apply after all to Orient as well as Occident. F. S. C. Northrop speculated that the Orient has had to acquire the aggressiveness of the West in sheer self-defense, while striving to achieve the happy synthesis of

> . . . a strong, independent nationalistic state of the Western type . . . with the minimum of repudiation and destruction of . . . traditional Oriental beliefs and values and attendant institutions.

But on the other hand some of these cases may simply have

illustrated what he called elsewhere "the realism of the Hindus." [19]

To sum up, the United Nations has been little or no help to the United States in actually overturning the *status quo* of communist power, (or vice versa, for that matter), although it has succeeded in sharply focusing public attention on the issues, as in Hungary. In Korea it blocked violent change and brought about peaceful change in the South. In Trieste it at least kept a light shining on an unresolved issue until it could be privately negotiated. The only way the organization could act decisively on other aspects of the cold war, however, would be if the United States were to back it up — or what would be left of it — with real power. Not being willing to commit American power to this end outside the United Nations, it is not to be looked for inside it. If other agencies can do it better (as when NATO legitimized the Federal Republic of Germany) it is all to the good. In cases such as Austria, the bilateral solution was regularized by admitting the country to membership.

The cold war in the United Nations has taken the form primarily of propaganda rather than action. If action in the legal sense was possible in the Security Council only when the Soviet Union was in agreement, it did not follow that action in the General Assembly would be effective simply because the Russians had no veto there.

Recommendations have been made, ranging from exhortations to condemnations. Apart from Austria, communist power has not retreated from one square mile of the territory held in defiance of Western sentiment in Red China, Eastern Europe, Germany, the Baltic, or the Sea of Okhotsk. The one act of "displacement" was the defeat of the communist attempt to alter the deadlocked *status quo* in Korea, but this ranks as collective security action, and was certainly not peaceful change on either side.

The United Nations has not dealt with all of the issues

reflecting the desire of the West to see the communist territorial *status quo* altered. Apart from the Czechoslovak and Hungarian cases, the central tension between East and West arising from the vassalization of the nations of Central and Eastern Europe, has appeared in the United Nations only in secondary shapes, such as the violation of the human rights provisions of the satellite peace treaties. The liquidation of political independence and human freedom in the three Baltic states has never become a real issue, although the status of Latvia, Estonia, and Lithuania is only questionably exempted by the provisions of Article 107.

The seven issues under the East-West heading have in common only the fact that they represented contentious or potentially contentious issues in which one side usually desired to alter a *status quo* that was running in favor of the other. The differences between the cases were reflections of their varying positions in the crucial power struggle. The Hungarian case was unique in that a clear-cut case of popular rebellion and military suppression by an alien power confronted the U.N., but U.N. counter-*action* was never a legitimate expectation.

In Germany, Austria, and Hungary the Red Army was actually present. It had ostensibly departed from Korea. So far as Trieste and the Italian colonies were concerned, the Red Army had never come close enough to enable the Russians to play more than a forensic role. Formosa was the only instance of non-communist possession of a territory whose status, already changed as a result of the war, the communists wished to alter still further.

In the colonial field the United Nations is able to take more steps that could be classified as action, for the opponents of the colonial order outnumber their adversaries in a setting where a head count can be as important as real power indices are elsewhere. Their cause is emotionally evocative and popular. And the colonial powers, far from always being filled with righteous determination to uphold their *status quo*, are sometimes either on the side of progress themselves, or cannot function purposefully in the face of an uneasy conscience, or are not physically strong enough to hold on.

Only in Indonesia and Palestine has the organization played a significant role in bringing about change over strong opposition. In Indonesia it supplied the modalities of peaceful change after the basic features of self-rule had been agreed to by the parties. The great powers, as well as the United Nations as an institution, had a bias toward independence, and the opponents were powerless to intrude.

In the other colonial cases where there was important disagreement no direct concrete results could be obtained. In Algeria, Cyprus, West New Guinea, and SouthWest Africa the responsible power in each case has largely ignored United Nations recommendations for action, where such have been made. In two of the cases the powers have come close to leaving the organization for good.

This does not mean that in these cases there will not be change in the future. But various sets of conditions must themselves change before the United Nations can effectively bring about peaceful change in cases of profound disagreement. Time usually alters the configurations of political problems. With changed conditions, whether they take the shape of new great power involvement or disengagement, or changed political attitudes with respect to a particular issue, the United Nations can potentially supply a framework for action. Lacking such altered conditions and attitudes, the role of the organization is difficult, and sometimes impossible.

Chapter 8

Present and Future

The great changes which have been taking place since the end of the war among the peoples of Asia and Africa must be kept within peaceful bounds by using the universal framework of the United Nations. The old relationship will have to be replaced with new ones of equality and fraternity. The United Nations is the instrument capable of bringing such a transition to pass without violent upheavals. —

Trygve Lie, *In the Cause of Peace*

The peoples of Asia today, of Africa tomorrow, are moving toward a new relationship with what history calls the West. The world organization is the place where this emerging new relationship in world affairs can most creatively be forged. —

Dag Hammarskjöld, *Annual Report*, 1954

It is no coincidence that the two chief executive officers of the United Nations should represent it as the prime agency for the transition of the colonial world from dependent to independent status. From the long-term viewpoint, this is the anti-*status quo* revolution over which the United Nations, given its ideology, its machinery, and its parliamentary complexion, is destined to preside. Here what is on the table is the established colonial order, and its disposition has become the first order of business for the United Nations.

Nor is this inconsistent with the Charter. Where Article 10 of the League Covenant was an explicit guarantee of the territorial integrity and political independence of states, Article 2, paragraph 4 of the Charter converted this positive guarantee into a negative one: "All Members shall refrain . . . from the threat or use of force against the territorial integrity or political independence of any state . . ." This new orientation needs to be taken in combination with Chapter XI of the Charter, particularly Article 73.

For if Article 10 of the Covenant symbolized the League's dedication to the *status quo*, Chapter XI and Article 73 bespeak the United Nations' repudiation of the colonial *status quo*, and they have been interpreted in this direction well beyond the limits the Western powers believed had been set when the Charter was drafted.

Today, the burden of proof seems to be on those who would insist that the forbidden land of Article 2, paragraph 7, has been invaded when the United Nations moves to alter a colonial situation, whereas once pleaders for colonial reform constituted a tiny band of supplicants who had somehow to demonstrate that the problem was international, not domestic.

The inability of the United Nations either to mediate the East-West conflict or, by itself, to prevent war, has sometimes brought into acute public question the very *raison d'être* of the organization. Yet serious crises arise from the impact of such forces as that of the colonial revolution. These not only affect the East-West conflict indirectly, but they have direct effects on the interests and strategic position of the Western alliance, including the United States.

THE THREE UNITED NATIONS

It helps to clarify these various sets of tensions and their relationship one to the other if the notion is abandoned that the United Nations is indivisible, in the sense that it supposedly deals with one inseparable package of problems, as well as the notion that if it cannot function effectively in one field, its contributions in another are meaningless. A more useful concept, one which the past ten years have increasingly borne out, is that there is not one but three United Nations organizations.

In the first United Nations, the primary issue of world war or world peace dominates the scene. But its role, by and large, has had to be one of spectator, propaganda sounding board, and species of political buffer zone between the two forces. It clearly can not and does not legislate the disposition of the holdings of either of the two sides. If continued support for the United Nations depends on its ability to accomplish goals which are beyond the reach of the nations themselves, it can have no future. But to insist on the ability of the United Nations by itself either to prevent a war that the Soviet Union might determine upon, or to engage the universal support of all states by specific prior military and political commitments to act in the event of war, however it affects their interests, goes far beyond realism.

The value of the United Nations in the East-West conflict in terms of peaceful settlement of disputed claims, peaceful change in the embattled regions, and universal collective security as a prime deterrent, is thus highly questionable.

While the United Nations operates on the basis of an unprecedented commitment to intervene in the colonial field, it has a comparable commitment *not* to interfere in territorial and other dispositions among East and West with respect to ex-enemy states. "Legislation" in this case would be a synonym for international civil war. The communist nations are in a seemingly permanent minority in the General Assembly, and what they desire goes outside the boundaries of the established order and the ground rules set by the majority.

The United States has invoked the United Nations in a few cases involving communism's territorial *status quo*. And, most recently, world-wide indignation over Soviet action in Hungary resulted in large majority votes in the Assembly calling on the communists to admit United Nations observers and granting aid to the hapless people of Hungary.

The United Nations can be of major value as a focus of public attention on such international injustices, and on belligerent or aggressive national and ideological policies. Also, it is hard to imagine a more apt agency for negotiation of issues where maximum publicity is desired. Finally, the United Nations has great (and little-appreciated) value as a site for private diplomacy, especially when national prestige and "face" seem to be at stake and there are therefore excruciating difficulties in communicating quietly in more formal settings. Daily and hourly propinquity in "neutral" corridors and anterooms paved the way for formal negotiation of the explosive Berlin Blockade in 1948–9.

But as a *primary* agency for peaceful change in the East-West conflict, a different order of evidence would have to be produced to change the present estimate.

The second United Nations, so to speak, is the functional organization which plans and carries out essentially humanitarian programs. The gamut of activity in the nonpolitical fields of economic development and financing, social welfare, health, education, trade and commodities, human rights, and so on, can be subsumed under this heading. It has overwhelming importance to millions of people, many of whom have never heard of the *status quo* and probably would not care if they had. From the standpoint of human and ethical values, this United Nations can stand on its own rationale, and deserves the support it commands from professional and lay supporters everywhere. The one point that is often forgotten, however, is that these programs can never be very far separated from their political milieu, however deplorable that milieu may often seem by comparison.

It is in the third United Nations that the issue of peaceful change comes into focus. This is the traditional area of interstate disputes, misunderstandings, claims, and tensions, involving societies that, while they may reject one or another aspect of the *status quo*, nonetheless are pursuing finite goals which, given appropriate timing and settings, can be negotiated peacefully. (It is tempting shorthand to say that this is the "free world" area, but it would be a solecism. Rather, it can be said that free world disputes lie within its bounds, as well as disputes among other nations that can fairly be called non-imperialist.)

It is here that peaceful settlement and peaceful change become operative. Even the Suez dispute, and the Arab-Israeli conflict that surrounds it, can be brought ultimately to solution. Violence smolders and often breaks out. Efforts are made to impose settlements by fiat or force. But the United Nations in this area does not hesitate to intervene, inventing new multilateral techniques — such as the United Nations Emergency Force — as necessary, to perform its functions. The only political condition is that the two super-powers not be directly involved.

In this area too the colonial problem is currently paramount. The most conspicuous role of the United Nations in furthering independence or self-government has been under the provisions for pacific settlement of disputes. Under this heading Indonesia, Israel, the Republic of Korea, and, in a special application, Libya and ultimately Somaliland, were in one way or another transformed into independent states. Ghana's election illustrates the role of "recognizing" independence.

Where people live within a framework of general agreement on the ground rules, and strive not for extinction of the established order but for a more "just" version of it, the United Nations' programs for pacific settlement, peaceful change, and even, in some cases, judicial settlement, become realistic possibilities.

There are ample suggestions in Chapter VI of the Charter for methods to conciliate and pacify situations or disputes between two states that are willing to be brought to eventual agreement. The passage of time often renders negotiable certain disputes that at one time appeared to be intractable.

But the goals of the parties must be finite, and there must be a deep-rooted willingness to find ways of avoiding warfare.

PEACEFUL CHANGE IN THE UNITED NATIONS

Three lessons of major importance can be drawn from the recent history of peaceful change.

First, peaceful change is rarely, if ever, completely bloodless. For this reason our definition excludes only changes that are accomplished *primarily* by means of overt military warfare. If there is bloodshed at the outset, but the processes of negotiation or settlement intervene, the change can still be denominated peaceful, whereas a change of territorial status brought about by military conquest in a war can not. This is no longer an age of aristocratic diplomacy, mercenary armies, or passive popular indifference. It is an age of often violent diplomacy and the emotional engagement of entire civilian populations. Peaceful is a comparative word. To be useful, it must connote a relative situation, not a political Nirvana.

Second, the progression from pacific settlement to military enforcement which bedeviled the drafters of the Charter — the so-called "chain of events" — seems today to be unrealistic as a general principle, although still theoretically logical. Peaceful change and collective security may actually be quite incompatible under present forms of world organization. To enforce a collective judgment without having the means to do so leads to unplanned violence. (This does not refer to U.N. forces which patrol, guard, and preserve cease-fires. These offer great hope for the future.) It has been true for a decade that collective security, in the sense of collective military response to an act of communist aggression, will take place first of all through the military alliances that exist for such defense, and secondly through the United Nations as an indispensable "umbrella" over the action, an aegis under which the strength of law and morality can be mustered and brought to bear.

But universal collective security in the sense of a blanket commitment to fight anyone, anywhere, anytime, on the basis of a majority vote in the United Nations, is unrealistic without the other elements that go to make up the sort of community that can and will support law enforcement.[1] Lacking a world authority equipped so to function, accommodation and diplomacy must replace enforcement in the sort of situation that arises in a typical pacific settlement or colonial problem.

The "chain of events" theory which once saw enforcement as the inevitable sequel to pacific settlement can, however, be thought of as applying to the peaceful change consequences of the pacific settlement process. If a territorial dispute is pacified but no change takes place, it usually means that decisive power is still on the holding side, or that power is evenly balanced, or that the issue will simply be reborn to plague the world.

The questions of when to accommodate, how to accommodate, and where to accommodate, must be determined in each situation. Revolutions do not always succeed, nor should they always succeed. But conflicts of interest requiring changes in the legal situation in order to establish a more stable, just and enduring world regime, are legitimate raw material for the United Nations. If political interests and political maneuverings determine to a large extent the outcome of a final vote, it is because justice can only be dispensed in this crude communal way under the present scheme of things. (And all things considered, it is probably a better way than through the politically irresponsible ukases of any seven wise and dedicated, even saintly men.[2])

The chain of events can still lead to the frustrating situation of abortive enforcement. This is one reason why objections to bypassing the United Nations in great power conflicts, or even in other cases, seem excessively doctrinaire when there is a better chance of reaching a settlement outside.[3]

A curious but natural result of certain successful changes in territorial status is the transfer of the dissenting force into the camp of the *status quo*. If by its rudimentary acts of creation or midwifery, the United Nations has dispensed justice to rebellious or disaffected segments of the world's population, it has not only lessened the tensions which such political malignancies breed, but it has performed an act of constructive conservatism, moving the people concerned to the side of the established order.

This is not to say that Indonesia will favor the economic and social policies of the United States or of the Netherlands, or that Libyans will not feel sympathy for their Algerian brethren, or that South Korea will remain satisfied with the *status quo* so long as the North remains imprisoned by communism.

It does mean that measurable progress has been made in the direction of stability, always understanding that new regimes of stability contain the potential for still newer tensions. Above all it means that the never-ending task of shoring up the peace has been faced and met in areas that had been radically alienated from the established order.

THE UNITED NATIONS AND NATIONAL INTERESTS

To think of the United Nations as something apart from the concrete national and ideological interests of its member states, is to risk misunderstanding the nature of its impact on those interests. Certainly there is a *mystique* of "togetherness," of common purpose and common response, which often helps to precipitate a consensus on specific issues, as in any collective enterprise. It is often helpful and necessary to set this presumptive fusion of goals against the particular interests of members, as the standard to which they should aspire and even conform.

But the particular interests remain, and directly influence the ability of the organization to dispense justice. In furnishing substitute solutions for the use of force, the United Nations starts from a variety of positions, rather than one. The *status quo* means, at any one time, Western civilization, the communist empire, or the colonial regime. (It is no accident that practically all the cases so far brought before the International Court of Justice for judgment were submitted either by European or Latin American powers, rarely by those whose ruling passion is dissatisfaction with some part of the *status quo*.)

Solutions to specific issues are arrived at — or rendered impossible — by the political combination and interaction of these several forces. While in theory the United Nations exists to serve the interests of all, those interests are in constant collision. If it acts to enforce a community will, that will must necessarily also be the will of a specific majority, and must be read to connote concrete interests in opposition to other concrete interests.[4] There are pivotal moments in history, as during the Israeli-British-French action in Egypt, or when Hungary was being brutalized, when there seems to be a galvanic fusion of interests into a common, and higher, interest. But it is in the light of the United Nations' role in the two principal long-term clashes — East versus West and, for want of a better equation, North versus South, that the satisfactions each group of interests receives or does not receive can normally be measured against their over-all interest in the purposes and principles of the organization.

The Arab and Asian group is enjoying an ever-improving tactical position in the Assembly with respect to its strategic ends. The failure of the United Nations to cope with East-West issues has satisfied this group's desire for *détente*, conciliation, and, at a minimum, avoidance of cold war collisions in the United Nations. On colonial issues it is riding high, with a constantly growing majority. This development is logically consistent with the bias of the Charter in favor of the revolution to which this group is dedicated.

The communist bloc would obviously be best served if the United Nations rigidly enforced its own self-denying ordinance regarding postwar territorial settlements. The loopholes through which the West has sometimes driven have left some scars. But neither the perpetual Soviet minority position on cold war issues nor the organization's military role in Korea have been sufficient to overcome the values which the communists have found in remaining.

Regarding the colonial battle, the communists are playing a game whose ground rules were laid down by Lenin. There was a time when Soviet Russia could pose as anti-colonial without hypocrisy. Today, if colonialism did not conveniently signify only the rulership of whites over blacks across blue water from Western Europe or its dominions, one might logically expect the anti-colonial majority to insist on debating Soviet rule of the Baltic states, for instance, citing as precedent the communist vote to inscribe the Algerian issue. The position some Asian states ultimately adopted to censure the Soviet Union in Hungary came as a relief to those who favor the single standard. The moment may still come when the communist nations will regret that at some point in their doctrinaire anti-colonialism they did not pause to ask the old, cynical question: *cui bono?*

To the so-called colonial powers the role of the United Nations in the colonial field is crucial. The walkout of the French and South African delegations at the Tenth Assembly and the South African all-but-complete withdrawal during the Eleventh session, should be read in the light not only of previous Russian walkouts, but of the refusal of South Africa to attend many debates over the years, the absence of Belgium from discussions of Belgian territories, and the general refusal of the administering powers to cooperate with a number of efforts to extend the supervisory functions of the organization. When the line is crossed on any issue into the no man's land of Article 2(7) spectacular resistance is automatically awakened, not only among the administering powers but, as their own interests are affected, among all members. The responsible Western powers may not go so far as to abandon the United Nations if they are pushed too far by the numerical majority opposing them, but this is by no means to be ruled out. Suez has critically sharpened this issue for them.

After briefly inquiring what "the law" has to say about the profoundly political process of peaceful change, we shall at last seek to define the position and interests of the United States.

The Legal Aspect of Peaceful Change

Men are not tied to one another by papers and seals. They are led to associate by resemblances, by conformities, by sympathies. It is with nations as with individuals. Nothing is so strong a tie of amity between nation and nation as correspondence in laws, customs, manners, and habits of life. They have more than the force of treaties in themselves. They are obligations written in the heart. —

Edmund Burke, *Letters on a Regicide Peace*

Chapter 9

Law and Politics

> Life and law must be kept closely in touch, and, as you can't adjust life to law, you must adjust law to life. The only point of having law is to make life work. Otherwise there will be explosions.—
>
> Arnold Toynbee

The concept of territorial peaceful change involves a crucial group of historical antitheses: stability versus change; the *status quo* versus revolution; and law versus politics. All of these represent, in one fashion or another, states of tension between the established order and dissatisfaction with that order.

The way in which men comprehend these tensions usually depends on their evaluation of the nature of man and his patterns of social behavior. Highly personal hypotheses concerning the habit-forming character of civilized social practices and, consequently, of law, often underlie the most objectively framed positions regarding the capabilities of the law.

The role that international law plays in the process of peaceful change is most usually dealt with by specialists in international jurisprudence. Analyses of this genre often rest on sweeping premises concerning the place of law in the scheme of things, and the habit-forming qualities of law in domestic societies, without always giving adequate attention to the nature or the utility of the political process.

Across the entablature of Langdell Hall at the Harvard Law School runs the legend: *Non sub homine sed sub deo et lege.*

Apart from primitive societies, mankind generally lives in communities that are governed by laws. The forces of anarchy that lurk behind the façades of organized human life have by and large been kept under control in municipalities and states by the rule of law. Before this standard men and their institutions are judged according to transcendent norms, rather than by relative physical strength.

But among the nations of the world the legend does not seem to apply. There are periods when the nations coexist peacefully, other times when their relations are characterized by cataclysmic violence. The setting appears to be significantly different, yet men speak of international law. Why is the leap from domestic to international law so extraordinarily difficult? What does it have to do with the problem of peaceful change?

THE DEVELOPMENT OF INTERNATIONAL LAW

International law began, for all practical purposes, in the sixteenth and seventeenth centuries, with the seminal writings of Vitoria and the Spanish Jesuits, Suarez, Bodin, Grotius, Pufendorf, and Vattel. Its creative impulse sprang from the need to impose some sort of normative structure on Western European society, rent asunder by the savagery of the religious wars following on the Reformation.

Like all law, international law had its ancient forbears. It knew something of Hammurabi and Moses. It shared the heritage of a powerfully fertile period of juridical creativity among the Greek Stoics, Cicero and the eclectic Roman lawgivers, Aquinas and the Church Fathers. The apogee of legal manual labor had been reached in 534 A.D. with the *corpus juris civilis* — the codification of civil laws by Byzantine scholars under the Emperor Justinian.

But by 1600 international law was not much further along than it had been when it consisted only of the rude amenities of the Roman *collegium fetiale*. As a set of rules that would guide the emergent national states of the sixteenth, seventeenth and eighteenth centuries in the expanding network of political and social and commercial contacts, international law quickly outgrew the almost superfluous references to divine natural law that ornamented the philosophy of Hugo Grotius.

Positive law took its cue from Emerich Vattel's repudiation of the *civitas maxima* — the universal society pointed most definitively by Christian Wolff. It applied itself to the practical matters at hand: rules of warfare, the marginal sea and territorial waters, the regime of the high seas, and the continuing need for standard rules for the treatment of sovereigns and their diplomatic representatives on foreign soil. In the absence of any supranational agency for enforcement of these rules, they were considered applicable only when they secured the consent, either active or passive, of the states, through treaties or usage and custom.

When early attempts were made to organize the then narrow community of nations for common action, the framework was eminently political. The Concert of Europe and the Congress system growing out of the Quadruple Alliance, originally joining Russia, Austria, Prussia, and Great Britain in a common front against post-Napoleonic France, operated sporadically but often effectively to enforce on nineteenth-century Europe its notions of the proper administration and distribution of territory.

Apart from their strategic targets — first France, and subsequently Spain, Turkey, and even each other — the three continental powers were preoccupied with the suppression of revolutionary movements to alter the form of government within territories in which they felt a concern. But this was not their only activity. The Concert also functioned to maintain the *status quo* in terms of national strategic interests of its members, as much as it did to preserve an archaic social structure under the Holy Alliance's principle of God-granted legitimacy. If what the Concert maintained was a legal order, it was legal only in the sense that it antedated any rearrangement that might supervene.

Yet in the same period a new spirit had infused the legal thinking of Western countries. The rationale of auto-limitation which positivist jurists, under the spell of nominalist ethics, had devised to account for the obedience of states to unenforceable rules, began to give way to a renascent naturalism, replenished with idealistic concepts such as Kant's categorical imperative and Hegel's ethical state. The *jus gentium* of the Middle Ages and of Hugo Grotius was ready to be restored around a new internal mechanism, whose mainspring was supplied by Rousseau's concept of the General Will.

THE DEVELOPMENT OF INTERNATIONAL LAWLESSNESS

The modern movement for world organization, world law, and world government grew quite logically out of a heritage compounded of the sixteenth-century revival of natural law, the rationalistic and optimistic spirit of the eighteenth-century Enlightenment, and nineteenth-century notions of inevitable progress and the perfectibility of men and societies through one brand or another of "social engineering."

But it emerged in the minds and on the tongues of men in an age when the same social and technological forces that had fathered the Enlightenment and its galvanic aftermath were coming together again in another climax, this time in the form of a series of mighty collisions between rival industrial societies. To the power of this historic impact a new quantum of intensity was added: the spirit of nationalism that paved the way through Europe for Napoleon's legions, unified nineteenth-century Italy and deranged it in the twentieth century along with Germany and Japan, and today intoxicates the half of the world lying east of Dakar.

The supreme modern irony is that this complex of forces of destruction and fragmentation was brother to the modern philosophy of international law. It was brother by the bar sinister, Cain to the other's Abel. Both were bred by the same revolution that has shaped the modern world.[1] The forces that have frustrated human ambitions for a rule of law were themselves spawned by the same sources that inspired modern international law and morality.

This parodox has created two profound dilemmas for modern political man. When he strove for stability in an epoch of revolution and change, the law came unavoidably to be identified with the *status quo* of the moment. But from then on it could never catch up with events. Peaceful changes sometimes took place, but violent change was more often the rule. Dynamic or rebellious forces characteristically had to go outside the law to fulfill their own laws of growth and development. Moreover, modern international law came to maturity coevally with the transformation of its subjects into independently powerful, purposeful, socially integrated, and racially conscious nations. So international law had to labor under a double disability: selective applicability because it was voluntary; and unreliability as a universal norm because by definition it represented the unstable *status quo*.

The second dilemma is more personal, growing out of efforts to superimpose a framework of organization and procedure on the anarchy of international relations in the belief that this framework could represent law. The ideal of international law and order has been an inseparable corollary of the modern liberal heritage.[2] Part of its creed was that all disputes between nations could and should be resolved by legal methods, by reference to an overarching legal order that, according to the doctrine, necessarily connects the hearts of men and nations. It was premised that there existed a true community of nations, that the League of Nations and the United Nations personified that community, and that, in the creation of international organization, a legal order governing the community of nations had thus actually materialized. These articles of faith were summed up in the opening phrase of the Preface to the United Nations Draft Declaration of Rights and Duties of States: "Whereas the States of the world form a community governed by international law."[3]

The present generation, once firmly committed to this optimistic philosophy, has had to expose its beliefs to the exquisite shock of two world wars. The chronic failure of the doctrine to explain satisfactorily the make-up of the political world or to provide a workable formula for maintaining it in equilibrium, damaged it gravely as an ideology, engaged as it was in an impossible competition with objective reality.

One reason for the increasing estrangement of this doctrine from the real world lay in the relative values that it placed on law and politics. Neglecting the profound truth that both law and politics are means to social ends rather than ends in themselves, law came to be identified with order, politics with disorder. Even where the political process at home was acknowleged to be the very vehicle of a lawful society, international politics was increasingly considered synonymous with the worst features of late nineteenth-century and early twentieth-century European diplomacy. Infected at the outset with the disease of power, world politics were seen as cynical, brutal, ruthless, and a prima-facie source of war. Thus stigmatized, international politics became the antonym of international law. In fact, in some eyes the effective role of law was to abolish politics entirely.

The price of even a partial detachment from the demands of this doctrine has frequently been loss of faith in the ability of law to order the affairs of nations, and of faith in the United Nations as that legal order. And, in truth, these articles of faith can be maintained, in their classic form, only with the gravest intellectual difficulties.

THE LEGAL ASPECTS OF PEACEFUL CHANGE

As of today, the political process, far from having been repealed, is in a real sense the only available agency for maintaining peace, settling disputes, building world community — and creating international law. Above all, it is the only effective means for confronting the omnipresent tension between stability and the demands for change. The law, which can play a vital role in making the political process tolerable, is sorely handicapped when it operates in a milieu in which the crucial cases are those whose resolution requires that the law itself be changed.

This question arose sharply in the now forgotten debate over the last few decades about the issue of "justiciable and non-justiciable disputes." This issue was related to the peaceful change question because it was international law's way of asking how it was to deal with claims that rejected both international law and the political *status quo* the law represented.

In the course of constructing the arbitral and multilateral diplomatic machinery of our century, this question had to be constantly confronted. A doctrine was evolved of the difference between legal — or justiciable — and political — or nonjusticiable — disputes. An entire spectrum of theories about the nature and propriety of that distinction came ultimately to be written in to treaties and international charters. The most extravagant of these theories insisted that all disputes, of whatever nature, could be dealt with by legal processes. In the Bogotá Pact of 1948 this theory almost acquired the status of an international agreement. It foundered, not on its fallacy that legal methods could solve all political disputes, but on the related fallacy that legal methods could be applied to disputes that went beyond the bounds of both the legal and political order itself, that is, to disputes involved under the rubric of peaceful change.

By 1945, when the United Nations Charter was drafted, the wheel had turned a full revolution since the beginning of the century. The Court would deal with legal aspects of disputes, and the political machinery would deal with the political aspects. There would, presumably, not again be a sortie by international law into the arena of politics, as there had been when the old Court issued its controversial advisory opinion in 1931 on the proposed Austro-German Customs Union.

In those intervening years, the arguments about justiciable and nonjusticiable disputes had paralleled, crisscrossed, and often duplicated the arguments about peaceful change, in terms of the search for an acceptable process of accommodation, within the existing legal and political order, of claims to change that order. It need not detain us here, except as a further demonstration of how hard men have worked in this century to adjust life to law, and how failure has seemed to be their customary reward.

Extravagant pretensions have sometimes been made for the role of law in the process of peaceful change. At the other extreme, the role of law is sometimes totally ignored, or at any event disparaged in favor of an exclusively diplomatic approach.

The willingness to abide by law seems to be the end product of a whole chain of social and political events, not the starting point. To expect nations consistently to act lawfully requires a generalized confidence, now lacking, that any losses they may suffer in one particular proceeding will be balanced out in the long run, as in any going legal order, by advantages based on the over-all protection and satisfactions a community would continuously furnish them. The machinery men devise to master international anarchy must be attuned to this crucial truth or the anarchy will continue to master them.

This, then, is our theme as we turn to a brief inquiry into the extent to which the United Nations — the contemporary agency for the "civilizing" of the political process — should be viewed as a legal order.

Chapter 10

Law and Politics in the United Nations

I am apt, however, to entertain a suspicion that the world is still too young to fix many general truths in politics which will remain true to the latest posterity.—

David Hume, *Of Civil Liberty*

There is one standpoint from which the voluntary, collaborative regimes that were set up in Paris in 1919 and San Francisco in 1945 can be spoken of as legal orders. Both were created by treaties, represented governmental undertakings calling for performance, and developed significant international machinery and procedures.

They were sufficiently imperfect, however, to give equal credence to arguments that, in the absence of actual governing apparatus, they could not accurately be described as legal orders; in the absence of genuinely common goals and an underlying value-consensus, they could not be called social orders; and, in the absence of arrangements to concentrate purposefully the power possessed by their members, they could not even be called political orders.

And yet of course they have been called all of these things. Both could be seen to possess a partial unity, but both lacked any transcendent principle of action other than the lowest common denominator of agreement by members. Because of these grave limitations, one is inclined to dismiss the organizations as orders, and describe them rather as voluntary associations of sovereign states owned and operated to maintain the *status quo* which reflected the present power and territorial disposition of their most powerful members.

In this sort of regime, legal alterations can be made only with the greatest difficulty, either by application of the doctrine of *rebus sic stantibus*, or by the amending procedure. But the burden of proof, and of aggressive remedial action, lies with the dissatisfied powers, and not with the community. In such a setting there is, traditionally, every likelihood of failure unless the major members can agree among themselves, or unless the aggrieved state can back up its repudiation of the *status quo* and of the existing distribution of rights with adequate power and influence.

As a generalization, this is too glib. It is true enough with respect to the League because it is now clear, through the chiaroscuro of words and silence, action and inaction, that the League existed in the first instance to preserve the European territorial settlement of 1919.

But the United Nations came into being in a world in which the wartime coalition quickly fell part. *De jure* territorial settlements were indefinitely postponed, yesterday's ally was unmasked once more as the enemy of the established order of society, and wartime enemy states were transformed into allies. The *status quo* was no longer something simple, like the image of the *ancien régime* that animated Metternich, Talleyrand, and Alexander I. The European political front of 1815, and of 1919, had been essentially two-dimensional. But the world scene of 1945 was a multi-dimensional complex of social, political, economic, and regional claims and counterclaims, full of such paradoxes as the assertion of profound hostility to the territorial *status quo* by socially conservative forces, and *vice versa.* If the United Nations is a legal order in the sense that it personifies the *status quo*, as such it has been challenged from the outset by those who in theory have the most to gain from such a regime.

The law in all its forms has always labored under what

Roscoe Pound once called "the perennial problem of preserving stability and admitting of change."[1] One of the most pressing questions about international law today is its capacity (or incapacity) to assist in the process of peaceful change. As the chief contemporary focus for international law, the United Nations is the central agency in which international law will function or not with respect to peaceful change.

Now much the same thing was said about the League of Nations in its heyday. One jurist wrote in 1933 that the beauty of the League was that is could formulate a "dynamic law" which would provide rules for its own change, whereas traditional law had been "primarily occupied with the static purpose of preserving the status quo, containing no rules for its own modification by a peaceful and orderly process."[2]

Yet the judicial body that functioned concurrently with the League — the Permanent Court — was bypassed on almost every major occasion. Its thirty-seven judgments and twenty-seven advisory opinions from 1920 to 1942 did not comprehend a single one of the differences that led to armed conflict or the unilateral use of force, such as the bombardment of Corfu in 1923, the Japanese occupation of Manchuria, the Gran Chaco War between Bolivia and Paraguay, or the Italian rape of Ethiopia. In its few successful acts of pacific settlement the League's political processes stemmed, not from immanent awareness of a law, moral or otherwise, but from objective political circumstances involving the relative willingness or unwillingness of the great powers to apply pressure when their interests were involved.[3]

The judicial process has fared just as badly under the United Nations. The role of the great powers continues to be crucial, and this alone points up the difficulty of making and applying the same law not to millions of anonymous coequals, but to eighty-one subjects ranging from miniscule to gigantic in size and strength.

Indeed, one writer who believed that "the purpose of the United Nations (is) to place mankind under the rule of law" actually prescribed the abolition, somehow, of great power status, as the *sine qua non* of a legal world.[4] According to another, the United Nations' actions are more political than legal, not because the political process is the organization's natural *modus operandi*, but because "The power of the United Nations in comparison with that of certain of its members is not sufficient to assure the maintenance of law by orderly and effective procedures." [5]

In the conviction that "the formation of the United Nations transcends all other developments in the law," [6] this attitude usually comes to rest on the assertion that "The United Nations should be a legal order (but it) cannot yet claim to be an adequate (one). Nevertheless, it is a legal order, at least it operates under and is restricted by a fundamental law, the Charter." [7]

Now, notions of international law are built into the structure of the United Nations at a number of points. But it is necessary to ask if these are, so to speak, load-bearing members, or simply a veneer that is freely detachable without affecting the organic integrity of the edifice. Is the United Nations primarily a political phenomenon, operating on, with, among, and under nations in ways governed by power politics, propaganda, and international morality? Or is it a legal order in the sense that it is directed at its institutional core by a principle that can legitimately be called law? Or is it perhaps a mixture of both, arranged in ways that confound the naked eye and often defy analysis?

The "impact of wishing on thinking" has tended to obscure the answers to these questions. Lamentably, this is true of both scientific and unscientific methods of analysis, possibly because the social sciences are still rudimentary to the point of frank subjectivity when confronted with ideological issues. Yet admitting all this, there are some tests that can be applied.

THE LEGAL CHARACTERISTICS OF THE UNITED NATIONS

The legal nature of the United Nations is usually described in one of two ways. The first, and more daring, is often so total and uncompromising that it clashes intolerably with the factual situation.

The other way is simply to catalogue the legal functions and attributes of the organization, making an empirical rather than a priori finding that the United Nations is a legal order.

Certainly a whole congeries of legal characteristics attaches to the United Nations. Its functional legal nature can be demonstrated by the fact that it operates in accordance with the Charter. The provisions of the Charter vary from specific commitments to expressions of hope, but there are those who conclude, even with respect to the latter, that because the language sounds legal, the provisions are, *ipso facto*, the law.[8]

The various organs are assigned certain defined powers. The organization itself now enjoys attributes of legal personality both in fact and in law.[9] In terms of law-creation, the General Assembly until quite recently was displaying energetic covenant-drafting capabilities.

It is also possible to quote from exhortations of the Assembly in resolutions calling, for example, for Progessive Development of International Law and its Codification,[10] Affirmation of the Principles of International Law Recognized by the Charter of the Nürnberg Tribunal,[11] and proclamation of the crime of genocide;[12] urging greater use of the International Court of Justice and acceptance of its compulsory jurisdiction;[13] and establishing the International Law Commission.[14]

An important body of legal qualities surrounds the United Nations' position as landowner with a quasi-diplomatic staff, operating in an international enclave within the territory of a host government.

There is, finally, a legally binding treaty committing the

members of the United Nations to observe certain limitations on their freedom of action, and to do certain agreed things. This treaty meets fully the traditional procedural tests of negotiation, signature with full powers, ratification, deposit, and proclamation.

In sum, there is an impressive array of legal, quasi-legal, and legal-sounding functions and characteristics that together add up to a formidable list. Yet none of them discloses whether the United Nations, in interposing itself between states in conflict, undertakes a legal process or a political process or both or neither. This function is the *raison d'être* of the United Nations. But it is still unclear whether the interaction of states which the United Nations examines, clarifies, disrupts, codifies, changes, or leaves alone, has thereby been affected by a process which can legitimately be called "law."[15]

THE TEST OF COMMUNITY

There are few texts in international law as authoritative as the one that includes this statement:

> International law is based on the assumption that there exists an international community embracing all independent States and constituting a legally organized society. From this assumption there necessarily follows the acknowledgment of a body of rules of a fundamental character universally binding upon all the members of that society.[16]

High on the list of questions that are constantly in danger of being submerged in a sea of metaphysics, verbal formulas, and exhortations, is whether the United Nations represents a community in any sense which allows one to speak in the same breath of law and its cognate social phenomena.

There is widespread agreement that law is a typical manifestation of a community or society, rather than the other way around. *Ubi societas ibi jus* is almost a commonplace on the subject of domestic law. But it is not so clear when one scrutinizes the United Nations, possibly because the framework and paraphernalia of the organization can so readily be mistaken for community or society in an unwarranted sociological sense.

The semantic pitfalls are probably inescapable, but it might sharpen the issue to define community in a way that eliminates at the outset the almost mystical bio-political requirements familiar to Germanic thought, once formulated by Johannes Althusius as *consociatio symbiotica.*[17] It can be acknowledged at once that the United Nations cannot meet the test of an organic community characterized by intimate spiritual and biological homogeneity (and probably neither can any modern social aggregation this side of Polynesia).

It is almost as futile to assert that any nation existing on this planet is *ipso facto* a member of a community. This often serves purely as a rhetorical flourish, but it also constitutes a vital premise underlying policies and programs, such as the Draft Declaration quoted earlier, and such contemporary statements as this one: "I will assume that there is not only a community of nations, but also a universal, although undeveloped, society of mankind." [18]

It has been said that the only essential conditions for law are the existence of a political community and recognition by its members of binding rules.[19] Still, if nations will not behave as if they recognized the existence of such rules, the first condition will not have been met.

There is, on the other hand, considerable criticism of the postulated world community. Edward Hallett Carr, who cut so deftly through the intellectual confusion of the 1930's, wrote that law, like politics, is a meeting place for ethics and power. International law exists only insofar as there is an international community recognizing it as binding, on the basis of a minimum consensus, and is "a function of the political community of nations." [20] He quoted with approval the dictum of a German colleague:

> All law is always the expression of a community. Every legal community has a common view of law determined by its content. It is an impossible undertaking to seek to construct a legal community . . . before a minimum common view about the content of the community's law has been attained.[21]

And from another source, in the same vein:

> Society is the means to an end, while a community is an end in itself . . . the one is founded on distrust, whereas the other presupposes mutual trust . . . Until international society is transformed into an international community, groups within the international society tend to do what they can rather than what they ought. This is the essence of power politics.[22]

Another view, denying the effective existence of international law, holds that international society does not today exist in terms of shared values. Thus, legal obligations allegedly arising from the United Nations Charter are meaningless in the absence of a social system to underpin them. The world is characterized by conflicts, but the intellectuals always hopefully postulate a mythical consensus.[23]

Even the author of the "Pure Theory of Law" acknowledges that a "community, in the long run, is only possible if each individual respects certain interests . . . of everyone else."[24] Without going behind this to the sociology of the law, Kelsen instead rested his version of society, whether parochial or international, squarely on the notion of force. Law is seen as a social ordering which depends on coercion, as distinguished from other social orders which may be based on voluntary association. Its fundamental function is to connect delict and sanction, crime and punishment, as condition and consequence.[25]

But the United Nations is far more of a voluntary association than a coercive social order, and lacks one of the sovereign qualities of power: a monopoly of force. It may be argued that such a monopoly is often symbolic, more presumed than real. But even on these terms, the national state seems presently to be the chief unit of political organization capable of sustaining such a monopoly, and that fact accounts for various phenomena within national societies in the fields of legislation, police powers, and the peaceful competition of conflicting interests.

In writings which depict or deny the United Nations as a legal order, the monopoly of force formula often becomes obscured. Some writers completely rule out the element of force in international law but champion the monopoly theory so far as societies in general are concerned.[26] This is paradoxical only until they explain, as they do willingly, that, like Hegel, they view the state as the *summum bonum* now, and, unless one misunderstands them, in the future.

The United Nations as a political entity enjoys nothing resembling a monopoly of force. The postulate of great power unity which was to underlie the collective application of force has given way, in the face of the great power split, to a more realistic voluntary program under the "Uniting for Peace" Resolution passed by the 1950 General Assembly.[27] Under this plan nations would contribute forces on a voluntary basis to repel aggression, which is precisely what they would do under a compulsory scheme, given the wide divergence of interests among the nations, and in the absence of a regime of government and law that would furnish all nations continuous protection against aggression from any quarter.

It might be argued that because the North Atlantic Treaty powers are all, with the exception of Germany, members of the United Nations, the latter can be said to command, at one remove, such power as the Western democracies are able to muster. This is only another way of saying that in a world where civilized state conduct is often skin-deep over the ethos of the jungle, certain nations are, to greater or lesser degree, determined to protect their holdings against assault. In an organization where friends and enemies, suzerains and their resentful fiefs or ex-fiefs, democrats and totalitarians all meet, true community remains an abstraction, and there is little present likelihood of the organization commanding, through its own standards and procedures, a monopoly of the power available in the world. This becomes increasingly true as a bipolar world of power may give way ultimately to a multipolar order.

But the deficiencies of present-day international organization, in terms of common values and a meaningful consensus about the way the world should be organized, appear most sharply in giving political meaning to such abstractions as international justice.

THE MEANINGS OF INTERNATIONAL JUSTICE

The members of the United Nations cannot be said to have a common understanding of normative, goal-oriented concepts such as justice. Justice for fourteen NATO members in the United Nations means, among other things, an easement of the basic hostility that confronts them across the Iron Curtain. For at least one of them — the United States — it presumably means the eventual transformation of the regimes East of that border. For another — Greece — it means ceaseless agitation until Cyprus, the strategic stronghold of another — Great Britain — is yielded up.

For the Arab members of the United Nations justice means first and foremost the extinction of the state of Israel. For those, plus another dozen Asian and African members, it means the liquidation of Western colonial rule in the great trans-Islamic arc stretching across from North Africa to New Guinea. For twenty Latin American members justice is an abstract good that should be invoked except where it may affect the specific interests of those states.

Finally there are the members of the Soviet bloc, fighting with unbending persistence for their version of what Carlyle once called "that great universal war which alone makes up the true History of the World, — the war of Belief against Unbelief." [28] To them, justice is a tactical concept which essentially means victory for communism. There is nothing new or startling in this atavistic notion of justice. The Athenians once gave the same meaning to it in replying to a petition from the Corinthians:

> . . . it has always been the law that the weaker should be subject to the stronger . . . calculations of interest have made you take up the cry of justice — a consideration which no one ever yet brought forward to hinder his ambition when he had a chance of gaining anything by might.[29]

THE MEANINGS OF INTERNATIONAL LAW

This reference to the cohabitation of communists and capitalists under the same roof suggests another test. The effort to find law in an international community that may or may not exist, is not made easier by reversing the equation and ascertaining whether, even if there is no real community, there may still not be law.

A cursory examination of Soviet concepts of international law suggests a negative answer. Communist notions of international law merely reflect the monumental clash between the Soviet and Western philosophies of social, political, and economic life. But they make it difficult to arrive at the desired conclusion by the back door.

Soviet views of natural law are widely understood. A few years ago Radio Moscow told its listeners:

> Morals or ethics is the body of norms and rules on the conduct of Soviet peoples. At the root of Communist morality, said Lenin, lies the struggle for the consolidation and the completion of communism. Therefore, from the point of view of Communist morality, only those acts are moral which contribute to the building up of a new Communist society.[30]

An anonymous wit once stated the creed with more

felicity: "There is no God and Karl Marx is his prophet."

Positive law is regarded as an instrument of the state and state policy in the Soviet Union. In the words of Marx:

> . . . jurisprudence is but the will of (the ruling) class made into a law for all, a will, whose essential character and direction are determined by the economic conditions of existence of (the ruling) class.[31]

The late Charles Beard was heard to say somewhat the same thing. But the Marxists have extrapolated the theory into the domain of international law, which, according to a Soviet authority, "is for the time being the arena of the struggle of two opposing tendencies — the progressive-democratic and the reactionary-imperialist. . . Like any other law, international law reflects the will of the ruling classes." [32]

As part of the earlier Stalinist phase of the current peace offensive, he was presumably instructed to concede that

> The reality of international law . . . is not precluded by the fact that for the time being there are on the international stage bourgeois states as well as feudal and socialist ones. Each of them, carrying out its own line and directed by its own motives, might be interested in supporting and preserving a certain amount of generally binding legal norms in international relations . . .

But it

> . . . does not mean that Soviet legal theory can admit the existence of a code of international law that would be equally acceptable to (capitalist) states and the Soviet state. The very substance of the Marxist and Leninist theory precludes such a possibility.[33]

The organic connection which ideology makes between law and policy was described by the late Andrei Vishinsky:

> The principles of Soviet law, reflecting the will of the Soviet people and its socialist conception of law, cannot fail to effect a decisive influence on all directions of Soviet foreign policy.[34]

Thus what is currently taking place is

> . . . the struggle which the Soviet Union is carrying on to instill in international law new progressive principles corresponding to the principles of socialist democratization . . . (the Soviet Union) feels that international law in the twentieth century is basically an instrument of policy devised and utilized by capitalist states . . . Soviet jurists take the position that much of international law is dangerous for the U.S.S.R. and cannot be accepted.[35]

Leading Soviet commentators frankly confirm this analysis:

> Those institutions of international law which can facilitate the execution of Soviet policy are recognized and applied in the U.S.S.R. while those that conflict with the policy in any degree are rejected.[36]

> The deeply rooted fundamental difference of the legal and social order of capitalist society on one hand and socialist order on the other entails a manifold and substantial alteration of legal norms governing mutual relations between the bourgeois countries and the socialist ones . . . the historical limit for the international law of the transitional epoch would be . . . the day of victory of the proletarian revolution in the countries of the capitalist West . . . (But even then) an intercourse on the basis of intellectual unity between countries of bourgeois and socialist cultures cannot exist as a rule, and hence the rules of international law covering this intercourse become pointless . . . (All that can be regulated are) values of the so-called humanitarian order (for example, preservation of antique monuments, prevention of epidemics, and so on — LPB).[37]

How is this policy applied concretely?

> As Vishinsky has denied that a court can be conceived as an instrument of justice above classes and apart from politics, so the U.S.S.R. has shunned arbitration and is alone among the major powers in not being willing to make even a formal bow toward the optional clause of the Statute of the International Court of Justice.[38]

THE POLITICAL BASIS OF THE CHARTER

The same doctrinal antithesis that bipolarizes general theories of international relations in this country, fixed the boundaries of nongovernmental thinking prior to the drafting of the Charter.

Some extreme proponents of formal juristic theory saw the postwar problem this way:

> To eliminate war . . . from interstate relations by establishing compulsory jurisdiction, the juridical approach to an organization of the world must precede any other attempt at international reform. Among the two aspects of the postwar problem, the economic and the legal, the latter has a certain priority over the former . . . the elimination of war is our paramount problem. It is a problem of international policy, and the most important means of international policy is international law . . . The idea of law, in spite of everything, still seems to be stronger than any other ideology of power.[39]

The total elimination of political factors in the postwar problem tells volumes about the rigidity of this brand of theory. But, despite the fact that oceans of blood were being shed at the time these words were written precisely because the idea of law could not begin to compete with "any other ideology," this rather astonishing view was not completely unrepresentative of its species.

The other extreme — the pessimistic, power-conscious, 'anti-utopian' school to which Reinhold Niebuhr had given its comprehensive modern syllabus[40] — was highly critical of the belief in what one writer derided as the "miracle" of international organization:

> While a system of law construed as a set of commands can be envisaged without any machinery of enforcement, it cannot be imagined without a legislative will deciding upon and defining the norms which constitute the body of law . . . the idea of international organization is unrealistic and delusive, and for that reason dangerous. It must be rejected because it arouses false hopes and thereby is harmful to the materialization of a genuine and organic order in international relations.[41]

The men who gave the creative impulse and the power of

direction to the United Nations acted somewhere closer to the right of this spectrum than to the left. There is very little evidence that the calculations of the three master architects — Roosevelt, Churchill, and Stalin — involved a significant awareness of or interest in the United Nations as a legal order, other than in the sense that the peace-keeping will of the preponderant coalition could brook no opposition.[42] They were simply acting in their capacities as political statesmen, at least two of them envisaging an institution to perpetuate the power of the three in a more enduring framework, the third aiming at aggrandizement of his own position in the process.

Community meant something different to each of them, and justice had a very special meaning for each. President Roosevelt, the only one whose government clothed this project in the language of law, should perhaps be seen in retrospect as simply paying tribute to the dominant American morality regarding international affairs.

One rung down the ladder, Senator Arthur Vandenberg, reporting on his attitude prior to the San Francisco Conference, said of the proposed organization that "it requires the creation of a new body of international law." [43] But there is little else in the record of his constructive and highly influential role to suggest that he ever again thought of the organization in terms of law. Instead, he was consistently preoccupied with four highly political propositions: an American veto on anything in the nature of a binding commitment; justice, with special reference to the fate of Poland; the concept of sovereign equality; and the means of institutionalizing the process of peaceful change through a political mechanism that could deal in a flexible and sensitive way with the constantly changing *status quo*.

The only other public figure on the American side whose influence at decisive junctures compared with Vandenberg's, was John Foster Dulles. A lawyer's lawyer, he too concentrated his energies on the politics of creation. Even in retrospect his attention remained riveted, like Vandenberg's, on the need for political machinery to ensure peaceful rather than violent change, relegating the constructive role of law *per se* to a minimum.[44]

It was only after the initial act of conception that American officials began to speak of the new organization primarily in legal terms. At the San Francisco Conference a more legalistic tone was introduced, partly because the smaller states were determined to encompass the rule of the great powers by weaving a juridical framework around them, partly because legal skill was called for to draft with at least a certain amount of precision (or imprecision, when that was desired) language to implement the broad agreements with which the technicians had to work, and, finally, partly because law is normally expected to follow on such an act of political creation.

But two years later Secretary of State Marshall was able to say to the General Assembly:

> The Government of the United States believes that the surest foundation for permanent peace lies in the extension of the benefits and the restraints of the rule of law to all peoples and to all governments. This is the heart of the Charter and of the structure of the United Nations.[45]

The genealogy of the United Nations suggests, then, the presence of three historical layers: the primary political conception; the "dressing-up" of that conception to modify it by introducing legal features that would, by being legal, restrain and even transform the working out of the original scheme;[46] and the development during the past decade of a living institution along a set of parallel lines that at any given time could truthfully be described, in varying degrees, as legal, political, legalistic, moral, immoral, amoral, cooperative, and anarchical.

MAKING THE UNITED NATIONS MORE LEGAL

The literature is replete with formulas for transforming the United Nations into an effective legal order. To do this, it is said, the Charter must be rewritten, and this time it must be law that predominates, not politics, or power, or power politics. Alterations in great power policies tend to stimulate this train of thought. As Secretary General Hammarskjöld said when there were first signs of a thaw in Soviet policies:

> Now that we may have come to a new turn, when we can reasonably hope that a real relaxation of international tensions will come to pass, it becomes essential to consider international law as a means of achieving rational and orderly cooperation in the solution of vital international problems.[47]

What is needed, according to one school of thought, is not more norms for states to follow if only they would, but tougher international institutions based on interests that are more clearly defined and apprehended than in the past.[48]

This suggests one point of agreement among most observers: self-interest plays a dominant role in the political affairs of the nations. The arrangement of power in the world has a factually determinative effect on the way states behave in concrete as distinguished from abstract situations. There also seems to be general agreement that the law as it exists today, whatever else it may be, is weak. But a multitude of differences arise over the norms that should and do guide the behavior of states, the way in which law is to be defined, the role it should and does play, the purposes and potentialities of international organization, and the expectations which men can reasonably entertain in the premises.

In planning for possible revisions of the Charter, many governments have shown that they tend to treat the question of law in the United Nations as merely one of a number of discrete, if overlapping categories. Law, as an isolated topic, finds itself pigeonholed as a coequal alongside such other parts of the whole as pacific settlement of disputes, seen essentially a political process; voting arrangements, seen as a means of measuring and sometimes simulating power; regulation of armaments, seen as a purely political problem of confidence and of political *détente* (and perhaps, ultimately, of law), and so forth.

It is consistent with this view of law to have isolated the juridical aspects of the United Nations in such clearly labeled outworks as the Court, the International Law Commission, and the Sixth Committee of the General Assembly. For the governmental policy planner, law in this nonlegal view is simply one of the many problems, most of them far more pressing, which necessarily arise in replanning the United Nations. Law, to an observer of Assembly action over the past ten years, is one of the less popular tools for dealing with disputes between states. In this category it is rarely confused with diplomacy or the processes of negotiation, and is often employed, in the sense of referral to the Court or the International Law Commission or the Sixth Committee, for its ability to delay and even anesthetize an issue.

A number of solutions have been offered which look to the institution rather to reform of human nature. One suggestion, pointing out the futility of attempting to project law far beyond the living and thinking habits of the entities it is designed to govern, recommends a gradual reorientation of the United Nations around the focus of human rights, believing that this will move the organization in the direction of the necessary "underlying agreement upon major values and objectives." [49]

And, in another thoughtful opinion,

> The United Nations Charter . . . can be variously conceived of as "the law" or as a framework to facilitate the development of the required social fabric which in turn permits the establishment of the orderly processes of the rule of law.[50]

CONCLUSION

The existence of significant truths on both sides of the argument, combined with the often dreary facts of international life, tend to devalue the normative type of analysis in favor of a more descriptive one. While every political problem the United Nations faces can, in theory, be viewed as a separate, justiciable matter amenable to legal solution, the same problems can just as readily be considered the products of a continuously shifting set of power-based interests, animated by political and quasi-religious ideologies, and constantly seeking a rough equilibrium which itself will solve some problems and create new ones.

There has been an unplanned and often misstated interplay between notions of law, politics, force, justice, and community in both official and unofficial thinking about the United Nations. The evidence suggests that the United Nations was not designed, except by those working on what a carpenter would call the finish trim, as a legal order in any sense which is evocative of such concepts as equal justice under the law, compulsory jurisdiction, legislation, enforceable contracts, and executive enforcement procedures.

Many contemporary students have perceived this, but some have themselves confused form with substance. George Kennan, while sensibly deploring the legalistic-moralistic approach to international politics, particularly lamented "the idea of the subordination of a large number of states to an international juridical regime," the imposition of a "legal strait jacket" on the system of relationships, and above all, the tendency of "the legalistic approach" to ignore "the international significance of political problems and the deeper sources of international instability." [51]

But this criticism is actually inapplicable to the extent that its target was the original idea behind the United Nations. The impulses that gave major direction to the American, as well as the British and Russian, conceptions of the United Nations were essentially political, not legal. The criticism should rather be directed to the dressing-up of the political skeleton to clothe it decently, as it were, for family consumption.[52]

The debate is further complicated by the disposition of some international lawyers to impute legal attributes to practically every political or social phenomenon, and the corresponding proclivity of some diplomatists to write off law entirely. But whereas the latter are characteristically cautious of generalizations, some legal enthusiasts, saying, with the poet Pindar, "Law is the lord of all," have proclaimed its ability to solve every problem that arises in the lifetime of a political organism, specifically the organism that is the United Nations.

Only too frequently the battle is between professions rather than ideas. "The most important means of international policy is international law." [53] No one would be more surprised with this piece of information than the people who daily employ the various means of foreign policy.

The "realists" have supplied a needful corrective by revealing the frequency with which political realities are sometimes unhelpfully disguised with the language and procedures of law.[54] Actually, the United Nations can most usefully be viewed as a hybrid — a mixture of different elements within the same exterior. It is first of all a political agency. The relationship between states, which is a political relationship, is carried on in the United Nations under a special set of circumstances that has important modifying effects on that relationship, but can still best be described as a political process.

What the United Nations can do with issues of great importance to nations involving alterations in the *status quo* must there, as elsewhere, be considered as a political rather than a legal problem, in a setting of widely divergent and often hostile concepts of law, morality, justice, national interest, and social and human values. And, having said this, we can now agree that the process does sometimes end in real law, rather than in an inapplicable and misleading legalism.

That a single case can simultaneously illustrate both points of view was shown by the actions of the United States government in the course of one short year. Its initial rejection of the findings of the United Nations Administrative Tribunal in the case of the indemnification for dismissed American secretariat employees [55] proved to some that this country is only too ready to throw off the law, mild as it is, for transient domestic political advantage. Its subsequent acceptance of the advice of the International Court of Justice that the Tribunal's judgment should stand [56] proved to others that the United States attaches an overriding significance to the legal standards of the United Nations.

All-or-nothing approaches to world organization and world law seem to be doomed to failure at this point in history. There is a need for concepts that will extract maximum social benefits from the political-legal order that exists today, and may still exist tomorrow and the day after. The ultimate emergence of a legal order is not precluded by history or present facts. It may even be possible to make progress now.

For instance, limited agreements can be reached about the way in which mutual protection from modern weapons systems and their unexpected use should be commonly viewed. "The necessity of living together has an educational force capable of overcoming the bigotry and rigidity of any theory." [57] Such agreement, based on genuinely common interest, can be institutionalized in a natural way that will, in turn, open the way to law. Such law would be built on real consent and would reflect community values that are real and not simply verbal, even if the nations remain hostile on a whole catalogue of other unresolved issues.

Whichever way one turns, there is no escape from the battle between ideologies that plagues the world as never since the religious wars of four hundred years ago. A yawning gulf separates the passions, interests, values, motives, and cultural patterns of East and West, North and South, communist and capitalist, Asiatic and Westerner. Is there still enough common ground to create a viable area of collective international action — and law? The answer given in 1919 and again in 1945 was affirmative. But it measured common ground, not in terms of real interests, but in terms of postulated interests, a supposed general welfare, and a hypothetical universal will to peace, justice, and collective order.

To create true law it is necessary to build from the center outward, which is a radically different mode of construction from the classic all-embracing sweep, into the center, of half-understood and half-meant commitments, by a variety of cultures that could not mean to act on those commitments in the way the public was periodically led to expect.

It is thus that our discussion of the contemporary United Nations is unencumbered with any particular philosophy as to its legal or nonlegal nature. For it is an agency where things, including things with the shape of law, have happened, are happening, and will happen, that affect and are affected by the changing contours of the political world.

And to demonstrate that the United Nations is not a legal order in the sense frequently employed is by no means to deny the effective existence of international law. There is international law for anyone to see who will. There are many legal aspects to the United Nations, and, in that sense, to the institutionalized problem of peaceful change. The United Nations has the capacity to change and to grow. If in terms of *lex lata* it is only an inchoate or embryonic legal order, in terms of *lex ferenda* it can become a legal order, if ever a real consensus could be achieved among the most influential members as to the qualities of a political community that must underlie any genuine legal order.

Peaceful Change and Foreign Policy

The real world with which the makers of our foreign policy have to deal is the temporal world of history, for which geography is the setting. It is a dynamic world, a world of challenge and response, a world of forces and counter-forces combining in their mutual opposition to achieve, at best, not the dead-weight equilibrium of a pyramid but the dynamic, precarious, shifting equilibrium of two elephants butting against each other. —

Louis J. Halle, *Civilization and Foreign Policy*

Chapter 11

United States Foreign Policy

> We must not think of peace as a static condition in world affairs . . . Change is a law of life, and unless there is to be peaceful change, there is bound to be violent change . . . there can be no true peace which involves acceptance of a status quo in which we find injustice to many nations (and) repressions of human beings on a gigantic scale. —
>
> Dwight D. Eisenhower, August 24, 1955

The policy that has been increasingly enunciated by the President of the United States and his Secretary of State is to the effect that the *status quo* must not be considered as fixed, that it must not be changed by violence to remedy its injustices, and that therefore peaceful change is the clue to the political future. This is not a partisan policy. In 1947 President Truman said:

> The world is not static, and the *status quo* is not sacred. But we cannot allow changes in the *status quo* in violation of the Charter of the United Nations by such methods as coercion, or by such subterfuges as political infiltration.[1]

This policy has a special application in terms of each of the three major contemporary tides — the communist revolution, the satellites' urge to freedom, and the anti-colonial revolution. Revolution itself has become a confusing symbol for the American people. The deep-seated dilemma over American colonial policy, for instance, stems from a moral issue: choices must constantly be made between deeply felt traditional values, and the strategic necessities of the moment.

Even when the latter prevails, choices must still be made from among different evaluations of our strategic position, increasingly in terms of support from neutral nations. Because the problem is complex and varies from situation to situation, no clear-cut and definitive colonial policy has been formulated by either of the last two Administrations. And indeed, there is no clear-cut and definitive policy that is applicable blindly to all situations at all times. Even when American policy appears to be only a series of "expedient" responses to differing situations, we ought to remember that it is not necessarily unprincipled. But the several principles on which it rests may be various and incompatible, and invariably some of them outweigh others in given concrete circumstances.

In the language we have been employing in this book, at least three important principles are at stake each time a policy is called for. First, the United States, as a matter of self-preservation, must defend and preserve the *status quo* of Western civilization against the onslaught of revolutionary communism. Second, the United States recognizes the necessity of accommodating the *status quo* to those forces of change that are armed with legitimate grievances, and that operate, not necessarily within the established legal order, but within the over-all framework of civilized society as we know it. And, third, at the same time the United States itself desires to see altered the territorial *status quo* established by communist power across the map of Europe and Asia.

In the over-all, these purposes are not necessarily mutually exclusive or even contradictory. But they have inevitably tended to moral ambiguity and intellectual confusion (just as the long-term American policy of peace and disarmament has at times been difficult to reconcile with the equally imperative short-term task of preparing for possible war).

The policies of the United States since the war have been largely successful in achieving a position at which peace — the absence of general war — is becoming a possibility. It is true that history has cast in doubt the precept followed so successfully by the Romans in the age of the Antonines: ("They preserved peace by a constant preparation for war." [2]) But the fourth dimension of all contemporary policy — the ultimate issue of war or peace — has undergone a major transformation that has penetrated all the other dimensions.

In 1943 Walter Lippmann was able to write that a policy of peace is an illogical national ideal because the true end of foreign policy is, after all, to provide for the security of the nation in peace and war.[3] But changes in the qualitative as well as the quantitative dimensions of warfare have demanded a modification of this otherwise cogent axiom. The doctrine of "non-recourse to force" has supplemented our other national imperatives in a way that earlier peaceful doctrines in the form of treaties and international laws, never could:

> The United States believes that whatever may be the differences which now divide countries, those differences should not be settled by recourse to force where this would be apt to provoke international war . . . We believe that the principle of non-recourse to force is valid not merely for the United States and its allies but that it is valid for all.[4]

That the Secretary of State could apply this theorem to perhaps the most unacceptable political *status quo* the United States has ever confronted — Communist China[5] — is a measure of the seriousness with which the peace-war equation is being reëxamined.

A leading newspaper aptly summarized the new situation:

> In general, most plans to preserve the peace have been based on the preservation of the status quo. This is not the essential purpose of American foreign policy . . . our goal is not only peace but also peaceful change under the "no-force" doctrine which bans violence. Both President Eisenhower and Secretary Dulles are well aware that peaceful change is the most difficult enterprise in diplomacy.[6]

THE UNITED STATES AND THE UNITED NATIONS

In the United Nations only some aspects of American policy are paramount, while others remain in the background. While the United States is "revisionist" with respect to the communist territorial order, it is more precise to describe this nation as a counterrevolutionary force with respect to communism's onslaught against the values of our society.[7] For, in the great battle between freedom and communism, the United States clearly does not behave as a revolutionary, except in the medieval sense of the right of revolution to resist change growing out of a prince's violation of the established rights of others. This is the right of people, as John Locke put it, to preserve what they cannot legitimately give away.

If we thus view the over-all Western position vis-à-vis communism as essentially conservative and counterrevolutionary, the Western dilemma comes into sharp focus. For we are confronted with the task of maintaining, against the Soviet Union, *status quo* A — the comprehensive Western position — while watching *status quo* B — the Western colonial position — in process of being destroyed. The paradoxes of policy, of strategy, and of logic all conspire to make the American task as complex as it is possible to be.

The inability of the United Nations to underwrite American dissatisfaction with the territorial position in Europe and East Asia is commonly regarded as a disabling liability. This fact usually underlies American dissatisfaction with the United Nations. But United Nations inability by itself to resolve East-West issues to our satisfaction can be viewed as a fatal liability only by misunderstanding both the purposes of the organization, and the inability of the United States to satisfy its desired ends *outside* of the United Nations.

In fact, as we have suggested, the organization has proven a significant if limited instrumentality even in the East-West sector — for example, in legitimizing the new order in the portion of Korea for which the United States was responsible, and in keeping the spotlight of world opinion on Soviet suppression in Eastern Europe. It has not inhibited and has in some cases helped at such times as this country wished to undertake constructive operations outside, as with the Trieste settlement, the Truman Doctrine, the Austrian Treaty, German negotiations, or the American demonstration of strength and determination in the Formosa area. If peace settlements such as the Japanese Treaty were made outside, this was entirely consistent with the limits of the organization, and accomplished the desired goals.

But the operational problem, so to speak, in the United Nations for the United States, is the colonial revolution, complete with all of its ramifications into Middle Eastern policy, the Far East, and relations with our European allies. Whether the United Nations' contemporary trends are harmonious with American interests depends in the final analysis on what American interests really are with respect to that revolution.

AMERICAN COLONIAL POLICY

The United States is itself a colonial power only in a minor sense. Its attitudes toward colonialism relate not to a problem it has failed to solve, but to a problem its allies have failed to solve.

We have spoken of the acute dilemmas that confront American policy in dealing with colonial issues. But while a decisive policy, applicable uniformly to all areas and situations, has not been formulated and probably could not and even should not be formulated, unless all the rules of government and politics are to be overlooked, few official policy declarations have taken the side of the colonial system:

> The United States is pushing for self-government . . .
> The United States will never fight for colonialism.[8]

If it were not for the cold war, the United States government, on the record, would probably adopt a surprisingly consistent position against colonialism and in favor of almost any program for its liquidation. Even in the cold war, it is only when a nation allied to this country by blood, culture, treaty, and generally common purpose — and this includes practically all the colonial administering powers — invokes the anti-communist alliance by placing its friendship on the table, that the United States has, always reluctantly, changed a colonial policy in the United Nations which it had felt to be right.

This is egregiously true on questions of inscription on the agenda. To be sure, American impulses on the rights and wrongs of colonial issues have on other occasions yielded to the necessity of renewing a contract for vitally needed raw materials, or of protecting strategic air bases, or simply of "avoiding unrest" in a tense world situation. But only a person unfamiliar with the military and strategic situation at such moments could have felt free to judge the policy unquestionably wrong.

As the United Nations penetrates more deeply into the no man's land between colonial relationships and genuinely domestic problems, the United States often finds itself in the equivocal position of seeming to vote against free discussion, and, presumably, in favor of colonial exploitation, but without entertaining those motives at all. A less responsible and far less demanding posture could be achieved by a policy of doctrinaire anti-colonialism (or, for that matter, pro-colonialism), perhaps generously reimbursing one side or the other for permitting the deception. This tactic is by no means uncommon in the United Nations.

Instead, from the beginning, the United States, for the best of reasons — because it had to be itself — has publicly exposed its painful and often stumbling efforts to do the right thing. No American need feel ashamed because his government was unable to slide into the happy decisiveness of a rigid and dogmatic position on a grotesquely complex set of issues. But it is necessary to lift ones eyes from the setting of day-to-day diplomacy to discover if American policy is in the long run consistent with the trends in the United Nations.

Few serious students would disagree that colonialism, as the institution the nineteenth and early twentieth century knew, is on the way out. The problem of peaceful change in the United Nations today is above all the problem of coping with this transition, keeping it relatively peaceful, and evolving new relationships and forms that will produce eventual stability rather than accelerated disorder. It remains only to ask if our own interests will best be served by assisting in this process.

The answer comes in two parts. First of all is the short-term element of foreign policy that has required this nation to look twice and even three times before agreeing to any action in the colonial field that might weaken or undermine the Western alliance. It is easy enough to assert that the Netherlands is morally stronger without Indonesia, that France is less disunited without Indochina, that Britain might be spiritually happier free of the embarrassment of rioting Cypriots, or that the anti-colonial revolution could become an adjunct of NATO if only North Africa were evacuated.

But no responsible American official could superimpose these prophecies on the concrete appeals of America's allies without weighing both sides with excruciating care. So long as political warfare is waged on several fronts, the rules for fighting a multifront war must apply. The center cannot be surrendered to strengthen the flanks, or vice versa. Each new problem must be evaluated with an awareness of the multiple claims on the American sense of responsibility so long as we assert our leadership.

Second, as episode after episode has demonstrated, the

United States cannot repudiate its own national character and heritage. Each area of American policy is like an iceberg, its stabilizing and enduring mass beneath the surface, formed by a process of accretion reaching back into time and the broad ocean of national character and history. Count Cavour once was quoted as saying "If we did for ourselves what we do for our countries, what rascals we should be." But we Americans like to feel that we are right as well as clever:

> One of our principal long-term assets is the fact that we are not compelled to make a choice between our moral idealism and our self-interests. We do not have to hurt others to help ourselves.[9]

A wealth of evidence supports the proposition that the United States can function successfully in the world only to the extent that it is internally at peace with itself, to the extent, that is to say, that its policies do not create a generalized moral repugnance at home. Because of this, the forays of American statesmanship into an earlier international arena were at times unsophisticated about how the world really functioned. Morality was substituted for politics, and proved to be an inadequate and even dangerous surrogate. But the answer does not lie in outlawing morality, the way morality has tried to outlaw war. Morality cannot be outlawed, and policies that are immoral cannot be perpetuated so long as the American constitutional system remains.

But while a purely abstract and perfectionist morality has led to hypocrisy and sometimes disaster, morality related to facts rather than fantasies is usually a reliable guide through politics. It must be pragmatic or it will be self-frustrating. It must be self-interested or it will inevitably be hypocritical, and thus immoral. In this view, political morality is moral only so long as it is constructive. Political immorality lies in the ordinances of perfection, in the rigidity of absolutes, and in the hypocrisy of self-righteousness.

History is neutral, and tends to validate the injunction of a perceptive Florentine:

> Let no state believe that it can always follow a safe policy, rather let it think that all are doubtful . . . one never tries to avoid one difficulty without running into another.[10]

As colonialism gives way to a new order of national self-determination and independence, still newer problems will arise and new challenges will spring forth, perhaps cast in economic and social rather than predominantly territorial terms. The residual forms of colonialism, as exemplified by the Soviet system, will at last be confronted and dealt with. If the United States believes in its own instincts and in its estimate of current history, it must either act with the tide of history or fight against it. The United Nations is with history in this cause. Unless we have lost confidence in ourselves and faith in our own political and social philosophy, so are we.

Thus the choice is not really whether we approve of colonialism, or whether, by assisting in the assaults on our allies, the United Nations is damaging American interests, or even whether we can stop this tide of events. The choice is whether to participate constructively in monitoring the process, stemming the tide when necessary and possible, and suggesting patterns of diplomacy, and political and legal modalities for assimilating the new entities to the camp of the *status quo* and stability; or to let this process of peaceful change be supervised by those who really do not believe in it, those who wish to exploit it, or those who are determined either to stop it or to accelerate it so that there will be change, but surely no peace.

Arnold Toynbee concluded from his survey of history:

> When a frontier between a more highly and a less highly civilized society ceases to advance, the balance does not settle down to a stable equilibrium but inclines, with the passage of time, in the more backward society's favour.[11]

This could be interpreted to predict the coming victory of communism (which Professor Toynbee specifically rejects), of anti-colonialism, or of barbarism in general. But prediction which pretends to foresee the future in detail is no more than what another historian called "the prophetic dogmatism of even the greatest second-rate minds."

The Hegelian dialectic advanced human understanding when it suggested that every situation contains its own inherent negation. But the Marxist version paralyzed truth by pretending to foresee the shape of the ultimate synthesis. The original situation will not remain unchanged, but this does not mean that its negation will necessarily triumph. The variables are literally incalculable. The era of peaceful competition opens vistas for purposeful action, and victory can be won in this setting just as decisively as it could be in a test of arms.

Chapter 12

The Era of Peaceful Change

To admit that there are questions which even our so impressive intelligence is unable to answer, and at the same time not to despair of the ability of the human race to find, eventually, better answers than we can reach as yet — to recognize that there is nothing to do but keep on trying as well as we can, and to be as content as we can with the small gains that in the course of ages amount to something — that requires some courage and some balance.—

Elmer Davis, *But We Were Born Free*

Hope, that which Gibbon called "the best comfort of our imperfect condition," does not entitle modern man to jump out of history. Nor does it entitle him to escape his own nature, and to pretend that within the human carapace he can ever avoid ultimately confronting himself. His social laws must conform to organic rules of growth and development, or progress will remain beyond his reach. The rhythmic alternations of challenge and response constitute a law of nature — and a good law — every bit as much as personal urges for social tranquility and moral perfection. Without those challenges, Rome suffered a "slow and secret poison . . . The minds of men were gradually reduced to the same level, the fire of genius was extinguished." [1]

The maintenance of international peace and security, history repeats over and over again, is not identical with the maintenance of the *status quo*. Progress, as Max Eastman wrote, "must consist in elevating the level and humanizing the terms on which the vital contests are fought." [2]

THE DIFFICULTY OF PEACEFUL CHANGE

The facts that have been accumulated tend to suggest that peaceful change is an enterprise fraught with difficulties, imponderables, and even impossibilities. Each tentative conclusion is subject to the contingency that peaceful change may depend on unworkable solutions. What are the classic conclusions?

(1) It is highly desirable to start with at least a minimum agreement between the parties.

(2) If there is no agreement between the parties, overwhelming force may be required to execute an imposed settlement or evolution.

(3) This being so, the old machinery is not sufficient and new machinery is therefore needed.

(4) But machinery itself is insufficient, so human nature must be altered.

Each of these conveys its own contradiction. If the parties are in agreement, multilateral diplomacy is probably not needed. If overwhelming force is required, there is no chance for success because such force is the result, not the starting point, of genuine international community. New machinery is useless without the will to use it. And human nature has proven itself uncommonly impervious to drastic reconstruction.

Hume evaluated this situation almost two centuries ago:

> Men are not able radically to cure, either in themselves or others, that narrowness of soul which makes them prefer the present to the remote. They cannot change their natures. All they can do is to change their situation, and render the observance of justice the immediate interest of some particular persons, and its violation their more remote.[3]

If this seems unduly pessimistic as to the potentialities of the human mind and the human spirit, it has yet to be disproven in terms of the observable date of international political life. So long as contending forces coexist under the roof of international organization, the organization's fundamental criteria of community, common purpose, and willingness to surrender national freedom of action and make both concrete and universal commitments, will remain goals rather than operative facts. Those who, partially perceiving this, recommend expulsion of the communist bloc from the United Nations, fail to appreciate the variety of revolutionaries and counterrevolutionaries who would still remain to confront each other (if indeed they remained at all).

For this reason the United Nations can never adopt as a consistent principle of action the total philosophy of one side or another in the struggle between *status quo* and dissent. When it does, its utility as a world medium is automatically destroyed. The shape of its operative principles at any given time will be determined not alone by its abstract goals, but by those goals as reinterpreted in the clash of concrete interests and tangible power outside the organization as well as within it. It must always stand for freedom, but it must never become committed to an inflexible territorial order, like the League, or its fate will be equally lugubrious.

THE POSSIBILITY OF PEACEFUL CHANGE

What is the role of the United Nations in this sort of world?

Its role is vital to the extent that it mitigates the naked hostility of clashing power, the use of unacceptable tactics by the antagonists, and, as with the colonial revolution, so long as it provides an agency for constructive rather than destructive change.

The essentially political process of resolving essentially political disputes must reconcile as best it can the real interests that are in conflict, rather than dismissing either one as legally unsound. Its emphasis must be on diminishing the harshness of conflicts between *status quo* and dissent. Peace will be secured only to the extent that the inherent tension between the two is continuously lessened and adjusted.

The United Nations can provide legal procedures and instrumentalities as the servants of the political process. But it cannot itself pose as the law, nor can it presuppose a consensus among eighty-one disparate objects of law sufficient to function as creator of universally applicable rules of law. The legal process must subserve the political process. If political decisions and solutions can thereby acquire legitimacy and the color of law, the means will have well served the ends.

In the cold war, if the West is successful in its short-run policies and Soviet communism decides to function as a primarily political and ideological, rather than a military, force, there is still no reason to expect a dramatic transformation in either the Marxist or the traditional Russian outlook on foreign affairs. To expect anything else undermines at the start any hope for a successful *modus vivendi.*

At worst, Western and Soviet power will continue to be dangerously juxtaposed along a lengthy periphery. At best Soviet (and American) power would withdraw from their overextended positions, with a buffer zone separating the two, whether it is a neutral belt of nations, a demilitarized zone, or a politically competitive region.

But to live in the same world with the Soviet Union is our apparent fate, however distasteful we find the prospect. Also in the same world, barring unforeseen reversals, will be Communist China. We will still need a supportive agency for working out our own destinies with our friends, for moderating the impact of our own enormous power on resentful, half-hearted, and otherwise "human" junior partners, and for defending with constructive and acceptable collective policies the political and economic system under which we live.

We will need an agency which can mediate continuously

between the forces of contrasting ideology, however peacefully they may coexist — a sort of political buffer zone. For the purpose of maintaining a political balance between the ideologically and economically disparate groupings of nations in the world, the political skeleton that is 1957's United Nations can in the fullness of time be suitably clothed to perform these functions better.

ENDS AND MEANS AND THE NATIONAL INTEREST

This study has maintained a consistently critical tone about the postulated "general interest" meaning a set of abstract ideals and goals where the wish is often mistaken for the deed. In the United Nations these goals have been premised as the common ambition and conviction of all the member states.

But these principles are invariably weak in competition with particular, short-term national interests. The ideal of self-determination was rejected by France with respect to Algeria, but it was also rejected by some of her most violent critics, such as India in the cases of Hyderabad and Kashmir. The ideal of immediate independence is rejected by the United Kingdom with respect to Cyprus, but it was also rejected by Indonesia with respect to the South Moluccas. The ideal of collective security was rejected by forty-five member states who stood by passively and let fifteen members carry out in Korea the commitment all had undertaken, but it had also been rejected by the United States in the earlier case of Palestine. The ideal of human rights is rejected by South Africa with respect to *Apartheid* and the treatment of its Indian minority, but it is also rejected at home by the most vociferous champion of civil rights elsewhere — the Soviet Union.

Are these ideals consequently invalid? Does no one really believe in them except as a tempting mote to scrutinize in his brother's eye? Do nations in their moral and legal attitudes behave as Burke charged of the disciples of Rousseau?

> Benevolence to the whole species, and want of feeling for every individual . . . form the character of the new philosophy.[4]

There is no simple answer. While men generally wish for these things with their hearts and souls, their governments find it necessary to act as though the goals were desirable luxuries, to be pursued only when permitted by the safety and well-being of the communities in their charge. This is not the way it should be, but the way it is. The dilemma of ends and means can never be resolved to universal satisfaction because it is fundamentally a moral question, its resolution a function of each man's hierarchy of values. But an instrument such as the United Nations can be employed for either moral or immoral purposes.

CONCLUSION

How then should we behave? What should we believe?

American foreign policies are not good because they are American, but because and when they are sound. Internationalism or nationalism is not good because it is internationalistic or nationalistic, but because and when it is enlightened. Liberalism is not good because it is liberal, but because and when it tends to the satisfaction of important human values. Change is not good because it is change, but because and when it spells true progress.

Faith is a weak reed if it relies on an all-or-nothing ideology. Men can honestly and constructively believe in the multiple values of the multiple United Nations, without blinding themselves to the anomalies and contradictions in the very notion of cooperative internationalism in an anarchic world. They can work toward the acceptance of international law without blinking the real-life ineffectiveness and inapplicability of law without real community.

The national state can be accepted as the present optimum of effective and efficient — and democratic — political organization, without glorifying it to the detriment of present human values or future international values.

The United States can be prepared for war and work for peace. It can confront failures in diplomacy, bilateral as well as multilateral, and still search for new types of organization, new procedures, techniques, and methods. Above all, it can work to create new building blocks of international community from which organization and law will follow.

Notes

Notes to INTRODUCTION

1. C. B. Marshall, *The Limits of Foreign Policy* (New York: Henry Holt, 1954), p. 112.
2. Arnold Toynbee, *A Study of History*, ed. D. C. Somervell (New York: Oxford, 1947), p. 556.

Notes to Chapter 1 — *THE IDEOLOGY OF PEACEFUL CHANGE*

1. Quoted by Herbert Marcuse in *Reason and Revolution*, 2nd ed. (New York: Humanities, 1954), p. 285.
2. Aristotle, *Politics*, Book II (London: Dent, 1939), p. 50.
3. Jean Bodin, *A History of Political Thought in the Sixteenth Century*, J. W. Allen (London: Methuen, 1941), pp. 426–427.
4. Roger Soltau, *French Political Thought in the Nineteenth Century* (New Haven: Yale, 1951), p. 34.
5. Edmund Burke, *Reflections on the Revolution in France*, *Burke's Politics*, ed. Hoffman and Levack (New York: Knopf, 1949), p. 290.
6. Herbert Spencer, *The Man Versus the State* (Caldwell, Idaho: Caxton, 1940), p. 69.
7. Thucydides, *The Peloponnesian War* (New York: Modern Library, 1951), p. 40. Or, as a pair of contemporary writers put it, the dynamism of history shows that every age has a natural aggressor, usually a young and growing culture, which has a strong urge to accumulate power, and usually becomes militaristic and imperialistic in the process. Robert Strausz-Hupé and Stefan T. Possony, *International Relations* (New York: McGraw-Hill, 1950), pp. 10–11.
8. Antoine Nicolas de Condorçet, *Sketch for a Historical Picture of the Progress of the Human Mind* (London: Weidenfeld and Nicolson, 1955), pp. 4, 10, 168–169. The impact of his philosophy was sullied only somewhat by his confession at the close that he considered his work an asylum in which he was immune from punishment by the facts of life.
9. Reinhold Niebuhr, *Christianity and Power Politics* (New York: Scribners, 1940), p. 147.
10. Hans J. Morgenthau in *Scientific Man vs. Power Politics* (Chicago: Univ. of Chicago, 1946), p. 203.
11. Frederick Watkins, *The Political Tradition of the West* (Cambridge, Mass.: Harvard, 1948), p. 128.

12. Geoffrey Gorer, *The American People* (New York: Norton, 1948), p. 60.

13. H. Lauterpacht, "The Legal Aspect," in *Peaceful Change — An International Problem*, ed. C. A. W. Manning (New York: Macmillan, 1937), pp. 138–140.

14. Bernard Brodie, "Strategy Hits a Dead End," *Harpers Magazine*, 211: 36 (October 1955).

15. Joseph A. Schumpeter, *Imperialism and Social Classes* (New York: Kelley, 1951), pp. 6–7.

16. John Foster Dulles, *War or Peace* (New York: Macmillan, 1950), p. 188.

Notes to Chapter 2 — *PEACEFUL CHANGE IN THE LEAGUE OF NATIONS COVENANT*

1. *The Record of American Diplomacy*, ed. Ruhl J. Bartlett (New York: Knopf, 1950), p. 461.

2. David Hunter Miller, *The Drafting of the Covenant* (New York: Putnam's, 1928), pp. 3–4.

3. *The Intimate Papers of Colonel House*, ed. Charles Seymour (Boston: Houghton Mifflin, 1928), p. 38.

4. Alfred Zimmern, *The League of Nations and the Rule of Law 1918–1935* (London: Macmillan, 1936), pp. 254–256.

5. See, for example, Wilson's address to Congress, Feb. 11, 1918, cited in Samuel F. Bemis, *Diplomatic History of the United States*, 3rd ed. (New York: Henry Holt, 1950), p. 641.

6. Miller, *Drafting of the Covenant*, Vol. II (documents), p. 10.

7. *Ibid.*, Vol. I, p. 14.

8. *Ibid.*, Vol. II, p. 12.

9. *Ibid.*, Vol. I, p. 42.

10. *Ibid.*, Vol. II, p. 71.

11. *Ibid.*, p. 98.

12. *Ibid.*, p. 107. Reportedly originally drafted under the leadership of Professor Zimmern as an anonymous "Foreign Office Memorandum." See Zimmern, *League of Nations*, pp. 189–208.

13. Miller, *Drafting of the Covenant*, Vol. I, p. 53.

14. *Ibid.*, Vol. II, p. 134. Cecil's marginal note read "this should be confined to territorial changes, otherwise it will be too vague."

15. *Ibid.*, Vol. I, p. 71.

16. F. P. Walters, *A History of the League of Nations* (London: Oxford, 1952), p. 718. (Chapters 3 and 4 of this work also contain useful additional material on the drafting of the Covenant.)

17. Zimmern, *League of Nations*, p. 241.

18. Miller, *Drafting of the Covenant*, Vol. II, p. 550.

19. *Ibid.*, Vol. I, p. 170.

20. *Ibid*., p. 202.
21. *Ibid*., p. 203.
22. G. M. Gathorne-Hardy, "Territorial Revision and Article 19 of the League Covenant," *International Affairs*, XIV: 819–822 (1935).
23. Harold Nicolson, *Peacemaking 1919* (Boston: Houghton Mifflin, 1933), p. 92.
24. *Ibid*., p. 93.

Notes to Chapter 3 — *THE RETURN OF VIOLENT CHANGE*

1. League of Nations, Twelfth Assembly *Official Journal*, *Records*, Plenary Meetings, p. 59.
2. The U.S.S.R. is not in the category of rebel against the *status quo*, ironic as that may seem. When it was tactically expedient the Soviet Union ostensibly joined hands with the bulwarks of the *status quo*. But otherwise it acted its traditional role of pariah, with a new ideological twist, posing alternately as a baleful hermit, a *tertius gaudens*, or a strange bedfellow, but reserving until its power was more determinative the role it now plays at the fulcrum of the stability-change equation.
3. Samuel F. Bemis, *Diplomatic History of the United States*, 3rd ed. (New York: Henry Holt, 1950), pp. 627–629.
4. *Ibid*., p. 639.
5. E. H. Carr, *International Relations Since the Peace Treaties* (London: Macmillan, 1937), p. 43.
6. Fifth Assembly *Official Journal*, *Records*, Minutes of First Committee, p. 125. See also David Hunter Miller, *The Geneva Protocol* (New York: Macmillan, 1925), pp. 28–45, and *International Conciliation*, No. 205, December 1929.
7. John Foster Dulles, *War, Peace and Change* (New York: Harpers, 1939), pp. 81–82.
8. Or one might style them, as in the thirties, "Have-Nots" or "Dissatisfied Powers." Hans Morgenthau suggested the "Imperialists" in *Politics Among Nations*, 2nd ed. (New York: Knopf, 1954), pp. 36, *et seq*. From a moral or legal point of view they were called "Outlaws"; historically they were "Revolutionary" powers; perhaps the most hospitable label is "The Dissenters."
9. Quoted by Robert H. Jackson, *The Nürnberg Case* (New York: Knopf, 1947), p. 237.
10. John Stuart Mill, "A System of Logic," *Philosophy of Scientific Method* (New York: Hafner, 1950), p. 326.
11. For instructive examples see T. E. Gregory, "The Economic Bases of Revisionism," *Peaceful Change — An International Problem*, ed. C. A. W. Manning (New York: Macmillan, 1937), p. 75; Frederick S. Dunn, *Peaceful Change — A Study of International*

Procedures (New York: Council on Foreign Relations, 1937), pp. 6–8; and William T. Stone and Clark M. Eichelberger, *Peaceful Change — The Alternative to War* (New York: Foreign Policy Association, 1937), p. 14.

12. Compare L. C. Robbins, "The Economics of Territorial Sovereignty" in Manning, *Peaceful Change*, pp. 43–54. Karl W. Kapp wrote in 1941 ". . . it cannot be overemphasized that the policy of post-war economic protectionism was primarily an expression of strong aspirations for national and political independence." *The League of Nations and Raw Materials*, Geneva Studies, Vol. XII, No. 3 (Geneva: Geneva Research Center, 1941), p. 62.

13. Stone and Eichelberger, *Peaceful Change*, pp. 31–32.

14. Dunn, *Peaceful Change — A Study of International Procedures*, pp. 10–15.

15. Professor C. K. Webster believed that the economic arguments were comparable to rationalizations advanced in previous periods of expansion: claims, that is, were justified by the doctrines of prior discovery, Papal award, effective occupation and development, strategic necessity, divine mission (and now trusteeship). "What is the Problem of Peaceful Change?," in Manning, *Peaceful Change*, p. 17.

16. In addition to Germany's claims on Austria (with the adjoining South Tyrol), the Sudetenland, Danzig, Memel, Eupen, Malmedy, and the Polish Corridor, Lithuania wanted to recover Vilna from Poland, Hungary wanted Slovakia back, Bolivia wanted an outlet to the sea, and the list could be extended. The Bolivian claim was the only one even tentatively submitted for multilateral action.

17. Adolph Hitler, *Mein Kampf* (Boston: Houghton Mifflin, 1933), p. 369. One is inclined to agree with Professor Rappard's estimate that: "No matter how generously the framers of the Covenant might have provided for the pacific revision of international treaties, they could not have made legally possible such events as the rape of Manchuria, Abyssinia, Czechoslovakia, Albania, and Poland. . . When the thirst for expansion is coupled with the lust of conquest, it obviously cannot be stifled by any bloodless procedures." *The Quest For Peace* (Cambridge, Mass.: Harvard, 1940), p. 176. Also compare the analysis of the French writer Raymond Aron. Writing of Germany's persistent failure to invoke any of the legal remedies during the interwar period, he said: "Germany almost never negotiated the diplomatic advantages she frequently carried off. Even when she could have negotiated peaceful revision of the Versailles Treaty, she unilaterally decided to abrogate the hampering clauses. To safeguard, pure and intact, the messianic expectation of total victory, all her partial successes, however they were brought about, just became past history all of a sudden." *L'Homme Contre Les Tyrans* (Paris: Gallimard, 1946), p. 33.

Notes to Chapter 4 — *THE FATE OF ARTICLE 19*

1. *Records of the First Assembly*, Plenary Meetings, pp. 595–597.
2. *Ibid.*, p. 53.
3. *Ibid.*, p. 580.
4. See Walters, *A History of the League of Nations*, p. 718; also Georg Schwarzenberger, *Power Politics* (New York: Praeger, 1951), p. 488.
5. *Records of the Second Assembly*, Plenary Meetings, p. 45.
6. *Ibid.*, p. 261.
7. *Ibid.*, p. 466.
8. *Ibid.*, pp. 468–471. The parties had engaged private counsel after the previous year's fiasco to advise them informally on their legal position. John W. Davis is said to have advised that under Article 19 a treaty could be revised only by common accord of the two parties; M. Charles DuPuis felt that Article 19 did not justify even preliminary debate of such an issue in the Assembly, and in any event Article 10 precluded revision of frontiers; M. Paul Fanchille's pessimism regarding the case was grounded on the absence of danger to the peace, such as actual armed conflict would *ipso facto* denote. See David Mitrany, "Peaceful Change and Article 19 of the Covenant," in *Collective Security, League of Nations International Studies Conference* (Paris: International Institute of Intellectual Cooperation, 1936), pp. 212–213.
9. *Records of the Sixth Assembly*, *Verbatim Report*, Sixth Meeting, pp. 13–17.
10. *Records of the Sixth Assembly*, *Official Journal*, p. 102.
11. *Ibid.*
12. *Tenth Assembly*, *Records*, Plenary Meetings, pp. 39–40.
13. *Ibid.*, p. 99.
14. *Tenth Assembly*, *Records*, Minutes of First Committee, p. 44.
15. The Belgians had countered with a resolution that was never voted on: "Every Member of the League has the right to draw the attention of the Assembly to a treaty which it considers inapplicable, and in such cases the Assembly, having by the ordinary procedure verified whether the demand made to it is well founded, will pronounce upon the merits of the case after referring it to the competent Committee." *Ibid.*, p. 45.
16. *Ibid.*, p. 100.
17. *Ibid.*, p. 56.
18. See H. Lauterpacht, "The Legal Aspect," p. 156.
19. See Quincy Wright in "Article 19 of the League Covenant and the Doctrine of *Rebus Sic Stantibus*," *Proceedings of American Society of International Law*, 1936, p. 68. But in the same article Professor Wright said that under Article 19, political disputes cannot be settled, or impending war prevented, or international law

changed, since these are done by Articles 11, 15, 20, and 23. "Rather it provides a political procedure for modifying legal rights in the interests of the world community," citing the analogy of eminent domain, p. 69. Pitman B. Potter similarly wrote that the word "inapplicable" in Article 19 "was not intended in itself to justify, much less to constitute, application of the rule of *rebus sic stantibus.*" *Article XIX of the Covenant of the League of Nations*, Geneva Studies Vol. XII, No. 2 (Geneva: Geneva Research Center, 1941), p. 12.

20. Dunn, *Peaceful Change — A Study of International Procedures*, p. 1.

21. Edward Hallett Carr, *The Twenty Years' Crisis*, 2nd ed. (London: Macmillan, and New York: St. Martin's Press, 1951), p. 103.

Notes to Chapter 5 — *THE 1930's: PEACEFUL CHANGE BECOMES AN ISSUE*

1. See Chapter 1; also H. Lauterpacht, "The Legal Aspect," p. 154; Bryce Wood, *Peaceful Change and the Colonial Problem* (New York: Columbia, 1940), p. 15; and *The Intimate Papers of Colonel House*, ed. Charles Seymour (Boston: Houghton Mifflin, 1926–8) Vol. IV, p. 35.

2. Dulles, *War, Peace, and Change*, pp. 49, 50, 137.

3. Walters, *A History of the League of Nations*, p. 717.

4. Sir Arthur Salter in *The Future of the League of Nations* (London: Royal Institute of International Affairs, 1936), p. 68.

5. Sir John Fischer Williams, *Some Aspects of the Covenant of the League of Nations* (London: Oxford, 1934), pp. 179–183.

6. Quincy Wright, "Article 19 of the League Covenant and the Doctrine of *Rebus Sic Stantibus*," *Proceedings of American Society of International Law*, 1936, p. 64.

7. Schwarzenberger, *Power Politics*, pp. 486, 488, 489.

8. Åke Hammarskjöld, "The Permanent Court and Its Place in International Relations," *Journal of Royal Institute of International Affairs* 9: 473 (1930). Josef L. Kunz, styling Article 19 "the real *sedes materiae*," wrote: "For the first time it has been recognized in a treaty that grave conflicts menacing to peace may arise out of the maintenance of what from a static point of view is the legally valid law, the legitimate status quo." "The Law of Nations, Static and Dynamic," *American Journal of International Law* (*AJIL*) 27:642 (1933). (Copyright © by the American Society of International Law.)

9. Pitman B. Potter, *Article XIX of the Covenant of the League of Nations*, Geneva Studies Vol. XII, No. 2 (Geneva: Geneva Research Center, 1941), pp. 57, 79.

10. League of Nations — *Documents Relating to the Question*

of the Application of the Principles of the Covenant, Official Journal, Special Supplement No. 154 (Geneva, 1936), p. 89.

11. *Ibid.*

12. *Ibid.*, pp. 90–91. While the French government did not submit any direct recommendations, the previous year the French delegation to the League of Nations International Studies Conference on the subject of collective security had agreed that, with adequately weighted voting in the Assembly, it would be willing to see Article 19 revised — but only if accompanied by effective sanctions. *Collective Security* (Paris: International Institute of Intellectual Cooperation, 1936), p. 200.

13. League of Nations, *Report of the Special Committee Set Up To Study the Application of the Principles of the Covenant* (Geneva, 1938, A.7.1938.VII), p. 96.

14. *Ibid.*, pp. 96, 113.

15. Quincy Wright, *A Study of War* (Chicago: Univ. of Chicago, 1942), pp. 345, 1075.

16. Webster, "What is the Problem of Peaceful Change?," p. 5.

17. John Foster Dulles, "Peaceful Change," in *International Conciliation*, 369: 493 (1941).

18. Stone and Eichelberger, *Peaceful Change — The Alternative to War*, p. 2.

19. Wood, *Peaceful Change and the Colonial Problem*, p. 15.

20. Dulles, *War, Peace and Change*, pp. 151 ff.

21. *Peaceful Change — Proceedings of 10th International Studies Conference* (Paris: International Institute of Intellectual Cooperation, 1938), p. 12.

22. *Ibid.*, pp. 18–21.

23. Webster, "What is the Problem of Peaceful Change," pp. 5–7.

24. Arnold Toynbee, "The Lessons of History" in Manning, *Peaceful Change*, p. 27.

25. Dunn, *Peaceful Change — A Study of International Procedures*, p. 3.

26. *Ibid.*

27. Walter R. Sharp and Grayson Kirk, *Contemporary International Politics* (New York: Farrar & Rinehart, 1940), p. 764.

28. C. R. M. F. Crutwell, *A History of Peaceful Change in the Modern World* (London: Oxford, 1937), p. 7.

29. Dulles, *War, Peace and Change*, p. 141.

30. Wood, *Peaceful Change and the Colonial Problem*, p. 26.

31. Lauterpacht, "The Legal Aspect," p. 141.

32. Maurice Bourquin, *Dynamism and the Machinery of International Institutions*, Geneva Studies, Vol. XI, No. 5 (Geneva: Geneva Research Center, 1940), p. 10.

33. Edwin D. Dickinson, "The Law of Change in International Re-

lations," *Proceedings of Institute of World Affairs* (1934), pp. 173–175.

34. Quincy Wright in "Article 19," wrote that great changes in international society "mark the failure of the system as a whole to reconcile stability with change," p. 62. He saw as analogous to the domestic processes of legislation, juristic analysis, etc., the alteration of international rights through adjudication (citing the League Commissions in Mosul, 1925, and Manchuria, 1931); through bilateral treaties; and by the great powers, as when the nineteenth-century Concert recognized changes in territorial and political status. See p. 64.

35. Dickinson, "Law of Change," p. 175.

36. Crutwell, *A History of Peaceful Change*, p. 1.

37. Wood, *Peaceful Change and the Colonial Problem*, p. 18.

38. As Quincy Wright concluded from his monumental study of war: "War has been the method actually used for achieving the major political changes of the modern world, the building of nation states, the expansion of modern civilization throughout the world, and the changing of the dominant interests of that civilization . . . The divergence between the advocates of change and the advocates of stability has been continuous, and the fact that each has, on occasion, found war a useful instrument accounts, in some measure, for the continuance of war." *A Study of War*, pp. 250, 255.

39. As well as other writers who have dealt only tangentially with peaceful change *per se*, that is, historians and jurists whose first concern was either history or case studies of legal change.

40. Wood, *Peaceful Change and the Colonial Problem.*

41. One of the few was Dulles, in *War, Peace and Change.*

42. See, for example, Carl Van Doren, *The Great Rehearsal* (New York: Viking, 1948).

43. Arnold Toynbee, "Peaceful Change or War," *International Affairs* XV: 34, 37 (1936).

44. Gilbert Murray, *The League of Nations and the Democratic Idea* (London: Oxford, 1918), p. 16.

45. Carr, *The Twenty Years Crisis*, pp. 168–169, 223. (A generation later James Reston was writing of United States foreign policy: "There is agreement that policy should rest in that middle area between intervention and massive appeasement, but nobody has yet found the solid ground between the two points." *New York Times Magazine*, June 16, 1955, p. 62.)

46. Dulles, *War, Peace and Change*, pp. 47, 138–150.

47. Toynbee, "The Lessons of History," p. 36.

48. Dulles, "Peaceful Change," pp. 494 ff.

49. At a Chatham House discussion in 1936, Mr. Toynbee said: "I think that a willingness to make effective arrangements for peaceful changes in the existing state of affairs implies a readiness to surrender the traditional sovereignty of the state by allowing the organs of the

League or of any collective world organization . . . to take binding decisions that may affect the states members' vital interests and even their territorial integrity." *The Future of the League of Nations*, p. 14. On yet another occasion he urged that the "Commonwealth solution" be followed, that is, "autonomy under existing sovereignty," in preference to a transfer of territory. In the same article he emphasised that the solution lay primarily in the colonial areas, and proposed improved administration, under League auspices, with greater attention to native interests. "Peaceful Change or War," pp. 43, 48.

50. Lauterpacht, "The Legal Aspect," pp. 158–164, 143. His later views have been selected as the fairest statement of his position. Four years earlier he had expressed grave doubts as to the wisdom of international legislation: "The existing *status quo* may be a source of friction, but there is no certainty that legislation devised to alter it may not prove even more dangerous to the cause of peace." He accompanied his customary prescription of lawmaking activity by judges with an attack on the *rebus* doctrine as "pernicious," and concluded that obligatory arbitration and compulsory jurisdiction for the Court were the real answers. *The Function of Law in The International Community* (London: Oxford, 1933), pp. 251, 255, 277, 344.

51. Dickinson, "Law of Change," pp. 177, 181.

52. Karl Strupp, *Legal Machinery for Peaceful Change* (London: Constable, 1937). In his preface to this work George Scelle, the pioneer of the monist school, deplored Strupp's approach, since any scheme, to be realistic, must be avowedly political, and not organically wedded to legal machinery. Scelle's own solution was to endow the League Assembly with limited supranational powers.

53. Sharp and Kirk, *Contemporary International Politics*, pp. 764–765.

54. Dunn, *Peaceful Change*, pp. 13, 126–128, 84.

55. Wright, *A Study of War*, p. viii.

56. Stone and Eichelberger, *Peaceful Change*, p. 41.

57. Crutwell, *A History of Peaceful Change*, p. 214.

58. Bourquin, *Dynamism*, p. 32.

59. *Peaceful Change—Proceedings of Tenth International Studies Conference*, p. 585. A similar conclusion was reached at Montreux the previous summer by the University Federation for the League of Nations. See *Problèmes du "Peaceful Change,"* Rapport du XIIIe Congrès de la Fédération Universitaire Internationale pour la Société des Nations (Lausanne, 1936).

60. William E. Rappard, *The Quest for Peace* (Cambridge, Mass.: Harvard, 1940), p. 485.

61. Webster, "What is the Problem of Peaceful Change?," pp. 20–24.

62. Wright, *A Study of War*, p. 1339.

63. Lord Lothian, quoted by Manning in "Some Suggested Conclusions," in *Peaceful Change*, p. 186.

64. Pitman B. Potter, *Collective Security and Peaceful Change*, Public Policy Pamphlet No. 24 (Chicago: Univ. of Chicago, 1937), p. 29.

65. Professor Dunn, looking back in 1944, wrote that peaceful change had denoted procedures for changing legally protected rights without war, in the belief that "it is possible to avoid all wars simply by providing a peaceful procedure for every kind of conflict based on dissatisfaction with the status quo." But "the only way in which it would be possible to put teeth into procedures . . . would be to establish a true World State." Lacking this, investigation must be directed at discovering the kind of cases the powers can be persuaded to settle by peaceful methods. "It is still outside the range of reasonable expectation to suppose that nations will willingly submit to procedures which would bring about changes in the status quo at their expense . . ." Cases susceptible to peaceful change procedures are found where conflicting interests can be compromised with both parties winning, and the problem is fundamentally one of persuasion. "Law and Peaceful Change," *Proceedings of American Society of International Law*, 1944, pp. 60–65.

Notes to Chapter 5 Appendix

1. But apart from the Treaty of Sèvres (which was revised as a consequence of Turkish victory over Greece in the Anatolian War of 1922), by 1937 there had been no revisions whatsoever in the territorial provisions of any of the World War I peace treaties.

2. The advisory opinion of the Court on the *International Status of South-West Africa* (*I.C.J. Reports*, 1950), p. 128, pointed out that the mandate to the Union of South Africa did not involve any cession of territory or transfer of sovereignty.

3. Dunn, *Peaceful Change*, pp. 84–107.

Notes to Chaper 6—*PEACEFUL CHANGE IN THE UNITED NATIONS CHARTER*

1. Quoted in *Postwar Foreign Policy Preparation, 1939–1945*, State Dept. Publication 3580 (Washington: Government Printing Office, 1949), page 12.

2. *The Record of American Diplomacy*, ed. Ruhl J. Bartlett (New York: Knopf, 1950), p. 624.

3. Where published sources are available they are cited. Unpub-

lished records used by permission of the Department of State are, according to the customary policy, undocumented.

4. *Postwar Foreign Policy Preparation*, pp. 472–483.
5. *Ibid.*, pp. 577, 580.
6. *Ibid.*, p. 269.
7. *Ibid.*, p. 584.
8. *Ibid.*, p. 597.
9. *Ibid.*, pp. 321–322.
10. *Guide to Amendments, Comments, and Proposals concerning the Dumbarton Oaks Proposals*, Doc. 288, G/38, May 14, 1945, p. 14.
11. *The Private Papers of Senator Vandenberg* (Boston: Houghton-Mifflin, 1952), p. 122. (Mr. Dulles took very similar positions, but has not recorded this history in the same detail. See *War or Peace*.)
12. *Ibid.*, p. 156.
13. *Ibid.*, p. 157.
14. *Ibid.*, p. 162.
15. *Ibid.*, p. 163.
16. *Ibid.*, pp. 163–164.
17. *Postwar Foreign Policy Preparation*, pp. 677–678.
18. *Ibid.*, p. 680.
19. *Ibid.*, p. 443.
20. *Ibid.*, p. 445. A Soviet commentary stated that the original American proposal "was directed . . . against the whole system of mutual assistance treaties which had been concluded by the U.S.S.R." S. B. Krylov, *Materials for the History of the United Nations*, (Academy of Sciences of the U.S.S.R., 1949), I, 112.
21. *Postwar Foreign Policy Preparation*, p. 445.
22. *Ibid.*, p. 682.
23. *Ibid.*, p. 686.
24. *General Series* Doc. 2 G/29a; see *Guide to Amendments*, p. 14.
25. *Documents of United Nations Conference on International Organization* (London: United Nations Information Organization, 1945), IX, 22 (Doc. 203). (Henceforth styled *UNCIO*.)
26. *Private Papers of Senator Vandenberg*, p. 190.
27. Krylov, *History of the United Nations*, p. 168.
28. *United Nations Conference on International Organization: Selected Documents*, State Dept. Publication 2490 (Washington: Government Printing Office, 1946), pp. 118–119.
29. *Ibid.*, pp. 128–129.
30. *UNCIO*, IX, 347 (Doc. 416).
31. *Ibid.*, pp. 127–128 (Doc. 748).
32. *Ibid.*, pp. 128–129.
33. *Ibid.*, p. 138 (Doc. 771).
34. *Ibid.*, pp. 139–141.
35. *Ibid.*, pp. 149–153 (Doc. 790).

36. *Ibid.*, pp. 419–420 (Doc. 792).
37. *Ibid.*, p. 178 (Doc. 848).
38. *Ibid.*, p. 249 (Doc. 1122).
39. *UNCIO*, VI, 359 (Doc. 785).
40. *Ibid.*, p. 410 (Doc. 944).
41. Which made it plain that textual exegeses bound only their authors, and no other delegation.
42. *UNCIO*, VIII, 195–217 (Doc. 1151). Of various interpretations by subsequent scholars of the Charter, compare some of the following: the Charter, while it makes no specific mention of treaty revision, encourages in various ways, including Article 14, adjustment of situations that might lead to friction. Clyde Eagleton, *Covenant of the League of Nations and Charter of the United Nations—Points of Difference*, State Dept. Publication 2442 (Washington, 1945). Since Article 19 had been "controversial," with "many" believing it had encouraged the interwar revisionists, to avoid the difficulties to which Article 19 had "given rise" no mention was made of revision of treaties in the Charter but it was "understood" to contemplate possible revisions. United Nations, *The Charter of the United Nations and the Covenant of the League of Nations*, United Nations Dept. of Information #27405 (New York: June 1947). Article 14 is "a modest approach to the problem of 'peaceful change' in a dynamic world." Goodrich and Hambro, *Charter of the United Nations*, 2nd. ed. (Boston: World Peace Foundation, 1949), p. 178. Support for inclusion of the revision provision in the Charter "was based on the realistic view that an organization established for the purpose of maintaining international peace and security should not be one exclusively devoted to the maintenance of the status quo," but because of considerable opposition, the realistic view yielded to the broad phrasing which was ultimately employed. Goodrich and Simons, *The United Nations and the Maintenance of International Peace and Security* (Washington: Brookings Institution, 1955), p. 228. But according to Schwarzenberger "The experience of the inter-war period had taught the draftsmen of the Charter the inseparable connection in any well-balanced system of collective security between the maintenance of territorial integrity and peaceful revision." *Power Politics* (New York: Praeger, 1951), p. 313. But again contrapuntally to this: "the neglect of the subject [of peaceful change] in both instruments is due mostly to the unwillingness of nations to endanger their favorable positions by making any binding provision for peaceful change." Werner Levi, *Fundamentals of World Organization* (Minneapolis: Univ. of Minnesota, 1950), p. 59.
43. *Report to the President on the Results of the San Francisco Conference*, State Dept. Publication 2349 (Washington: Government Printing Office, 1945), pp. 58–59. Speaking of Article 109 and the

amending process, the Report stated: "Those who seek to develop procedures for the peaceful settlement of international disputes always confront the hard task of striking a balance between the necessity of assuring stability and security on the one hand and of providing room for growth and adaptation on the other." It then described the amending process adopted as a compromise between "those who feared lest the status quo be permanently frozen" and those who wanted to ensure that the rights and duties under the Charter would not "be brought into a different balance from that which Members had originally accepted." p. 166.

44. *Hearings Before the Senate Committee on Foreign Relations on the Charter of the United Nations* (Washington: Government Printing Office, 1945), p. 218.

45. *Ibid.*, pp. 249–252.

46. Duff Cooper, in his memoirs, *Old Men Forget* (New York: Dutton, 1954), p. 194.

Notes to Chapter 7 — *THE PAST: 1945 TO 1957*

1. Karl Marx, in Marx and Engels, *Works* (Russian ed.), ix, p. 372.

2. *A Decade of American Foreign Policy, Basic Documents, 1941–1949*, Senate Committee on Foreign Relations, 81st Congress, 1st Sess., Doc. No. 123 (Washington: Government Printing Office, 1950), p. 29.

3. See John H. Kautsky, "The New Strategy of International Communism," 49 *American Political Science Review* (1955).

4. Sir Halford Mackinder, "Who rules the World-Island commands the World," *Democratic Ideals and Reality* (New York: Holt, 1919), p. 150.

5. *The Education of Henry Adams* (New York: Modern Library, 1931), p. 479.

6. Cameroons (France), Cameroons (U.K.), New Guinea (Australia), Nauru (Australia *et al.*), Pacific Islands (U.S.), Ruanda-Urundi (Belgium), Somaliland (Italy), Tanganyika (U.K.), Togoland (France), Togoland (U.K.), and Western Samoa (New Zealand).

7. The figure 100,000,000 is given in the *Report by the President to Congress for 1955: U.S. Participation in the U.N.*, State Dept. Publication 6318 (Washington: Government Printing Office, 1956), p. 176. The Senate Committee on Foreign Relations used the figure 120,000,000 in Staff Study No. 9, *The United Nations and Dependent Territories* (Washington: Government Printing Office, 1955), p. 6. General Assembly Resolution 66 (I) of Dec. 14, 1946, listed seventy-four territories as to which administering authorities had indicated they would transmit information. *U.N.Doc.* A/64/Add.1, pp. 124–6. A list of all the territories on which reports have been made is contained in Sen-

ate Committee on Foreign Relations, *Review of the United Nations Charter — A Collection of Documents*, 83rd Congress, 2nd Sess., Doc. No. 87 (Washington: Government Printing Office, 1954), p. 726.

8. See United Nations, *Repertory of Practice of United Nations Organs*, I, 465–468 (U.N. 1955. V2, Vol. 1). Also *Official Records* of Assembly (Second, Sixth, Seventh, and Eighth Sessions, and of *Ad Hoc* Committee on Palestine).

9. Former President Hoover recently publicly deplored the failure of the Charter to embody his original suggestion for machinery "for the revision of onerous treaties. Intolerable treaties often go on and on," he stated, "infecting the world, when there is a general conclusion that they are outmoded." Apparently alluding to Senator Vandenberg's cherished phrase "regardless of origin," Mr. Hoover concluded, "There are some indefinite words which really do not mean very much." *Hearings Before Subcommittee of Senate Committee on Foreign Relations on Review of the United Nations Charter*, Part 12 (Washington: Government Printing Office, 1955), p. 1743.

10. The word "action," although useful, is imprecise, since only the Security Council is technically capable of action while the Assembly can only recommend.

11. See *Report by the President to the Congress on U.S. Participation in the U.N.*, 1950. State Dept. Publication 4178 (Washington: Government Printing Office, 1951), pp. 94–95.

12. The cases are conveniently summarized in the series of annual *Reports by the President to the Congress on U.S. Participation in the U.N.*, in print for the years 1946 through 1955. State Dept. Publications No. 2735, 3024, 3437, 3765, 4178, 4583, 5034, 5459, 5769, and 6318. (Washington: Government Printing Office, ———.) Also compare *United Nations Yearbooks*.

13. *Report by the President*, 1952, p. 184.

14. General Assembly Resolution 849 (IX), *U.N. Doc.* A/2890, pp. 27–28.

15. See also General Assembly Resolutions 558 (VI), *U.N. Doc.* A/2119, pp. 57–58, and 752 (VIII), *U.N. Doc.* A/2360, p. 30.

16. *I.C.J. Yearbook* 1953–1954 (Leyden: Sijthoff, 1954), pp. 77–80. Out of eight advisory opinions to date, only the SouthWest Africa cases involved peaceful change (unless it be argued that the membership question is closely enough related to the problem of peaceful territorial change to add to the list the advisory opinion regarding Article 4 of the Charter. There is some force to the argument, but it seems sufficiently on the side of *lex ferenda* to omit from consideration here).

17. The South African delegate, in explaining his delegation's walkout in the 1955 Assembly, characterized the attacks over the years on South African racial and other policies as "incitement tending to up-

set order, law and good government." *New York Times*, Nov. 10, 1955.

18. As a Belgian authority indignantly commented "If the foreign authority happens to be a colored people, nobody dreams of condemning this form of colonialism." Pierre Ryckmans, "Belgian Colonialism," *Foreign Affairs* 34:93 (1955).

19. F. S. C. Northrup, *The Meeting of East and West* (New York: Macmillian, 1946), pp. 419, 380.

Notes to Chapter 8 — *PRESENT AND FUTURE*

1. Gerhart Niemeyer said it well: "the essential prerequisites for a society, a monopoly of force and a broad consensus about the uses of such centralized force, do not exist on a world scale. This means that any rational approach to the problem of international order must take fully into account the existence of a multitude of centers, each capable of exercising a certain amount of ordering functions." "Doctrines on International Relations," *World Politics* IV: 290 (1952).

2. As suggested by Sir Alfred Zimmern, *The American Road to World Peace* (New York: Dutton, 1953), pp. 237–238.

3. The American Association for the United Nations recently stated publicly: "A danger to the United Nations and to the peace of the world would be a tendency of the great powers to bypass the United Nations for local or regional arrangements or settlements." Reported in *New York Times*, June 12, 1955.

4. In this connection, see Stanley Hoffman's thesis that the Concert suffered because, by subjecting small powers to the will of great powers, no disinterested third parties were left in the organization itself, with the result that the powers viewed crises only in terms of their own interests. *Organizations Internationales et Pouvoir Politiques Des États* (Paris: Libraire Armand Colin, 1954), p. 116.

Notes to Chapter 9 — *LAW AND POLITICS*

1. One important connection in this sequence was made by J. L. Talmon in *The Rise of Totalitarian Democracy* (Boston: Beacon, 1952).

2. "The ideal of Liberalism in international affairs is that the nations should transcend the phase of political rivalry, should live together in peace, and, by the active and free exchange of economic and cultural goods, should satisfy each other's needs and develop in the best way their respective talents." Guido de Ruggiero, *The History of European Liberalism* (London: Oxford, 1927), p. 412.

3. *U.N. Doc.* A/1251, p. 67.

Notes to Chapter 10 — *LAW AND POLITICS IN THE UNITED NATIONS*

1. Roscoe Pound, *An Introduction to the Philosophy of Law* (New Haven: Yale, 1922), p. 30.
2. Josef L. Kunz, "The Law of Nations, Static and Dynamic," *American Journal of International Law* (*AJIL*) 27:630 (1933).
3. G. Niemeyer, "The Balance Sheet of the League Experiment," *International Organization* VI, esp. 546 (1952).
4. Zimmern, *The American Road*, p. 255.
5. Quincy Wright, *Law and Politics in the World Community*, ed. G. A. Lipsky (Berkeley: Univ. of Calif., 1953), p. 13.
6. Charles Fahy, "Legal Aspects of the Work of the United Nations," *Illinois Law Review* 43:135 (1948).
7. Eagleton, "The United Nations: A Legal Order?," *Law and Politics in the World Community*, p. 134. See also his "The Yardstick of International Law," *The Annals of the American Academy of Political and Social Science* (November 1954), pp. 68, 76. The late A. H. Feller wrote: "The United Nations is a legal order and it can not tear itself loose from the specific restrictions of the Charter, irksome though they may be from time to time to one interest or another," *The United Nations and World Community* (Boston: Little, Brown, 1952), p. 43.
8. H. Lauterpacht, *International Law and Human Rights* (London: Stevens, 1950), p. 34.
9. See Advisory Opinion, *Reparations for Injuries Suffered in the Service of the U.N.* (*I.C.J. Reports*, 1949), p. 174.
10. General Assembly Resolution 94 (I), 1946, *U.N.Doc.* A/64/Add. 1, p. 187.
11. General Assembly Resolution 95 (I), *Ibid.*, p. 188.
12. General Assembly Resolution 96 (I), *Ibid.*, pp. 188–189.
13. General Assembly Resolution 171 (II), 1947, *U.N.Doc.* A/519, p. 103.
14. General Assembly Resolution 174 (II), *Ibid.*, pp. 103–104.
15. One French view, dedicated to the principle of law, for that reason rejects rather than affirms the legal nature of the United Nations. A. Salomon, *L'O.N.U. et la Paix* (Paris: Les Editions Internationales, 1948).
16. Oppenheim, *International Law*, 6th ed., H. Lauterpacht, I, 48.
17. *Politica Methodica Digesta*, trans. C. J. Friedrich (Cambridge, Mass.: Harvard, 1932).
18. Wright, *Law and Politics*, p. 6.
19. Sir Frederick Pollock, quoted in J. L. Brierly, *The Law of Nations*, 4th ed. (London: Oxford, 1949), p. 71.
20. Carr, *The Twenty Years Crisis*, p. 178.

21. F. Berber, quoted in Carr, *The Twenty Years Crisis*, p. 177.
22. Schwarzenberger, *Power Politics*, pp. 12–13.
23. P. E. Corbett, *Law and Society in the Relations of States* (New York: Harcourt, Brace, 1951), pp. 42, 52.
24. Hans Kelsen, *Law and Peace in International Relations* (Cambridge, Mass.: Harvard, 1942), p. 13.
25. *Ibid.*, pp. 7, 12, 26.
26. For example, Gerhart Niemeyer, *Law Without Force* (Princeton, N. J.: Princeton, 1941).
27. General Assembly Resolution 377(V), *U.N.Doc.* A/1775, pp. 10–12.
28. Carlyle, *On Heroes and Hero-Worship* (London: Dent, 1954), p. 430.
29. Thucydides, *The Peloponnesian War* (New York: Modern Library, 1951), p. 44.
30. Aug. 20, 1950. Quoted in *The Kremlin Speaks*, State Dept. Publication 4264 (1951).
31. Marx, *Selected Works* (1935). Quoted by John N. Hazard in "The Soviet Union and International Law," *Illinois Law Review*, 43:592 (1948). Some points of similarity between socialist and "bourgeois" international law were outlined by W. W. Kulski, "The Soviet Interpretation of International Law," *AJIL*, 49 (1955).
32. Prof. E. A. Korovin, quoted by Mintauts Chakste in *AJIL*, 43:21, 29–30 (1949).
33. *Ibid.*
34. Quoted by Hazard, "Soviet Union," p. 592.
35. *Ibid.*, pp. 599, 606.
36. Prof. F. I. Kozhevnikov, 1948, as translated by John N. Hazard, *AJIL*, 44:215 (1950).
37. Korovin, *AJIL*, 43:26–27 (1949).
38. Rupert Emerson and Inis L. Claude, Jr., "The Soviet Union and the United Nations," *International Organization*, VI:4 (1952).
39. Hans Kelsen, "Compulsory Arbitration of International Disputes," *AJIL*, 37:397–399 (1943).
40. Reinhold Niebuhr, *Moral Man and Immoral Society* (New York: Scribners, 1934).
41. Niemeyer, *Law Without Force*, pp. 393–394.
42. See especially Robert E. Sherwood, *Roosevelt and Hopkins* (New York: Harper, 1948), and Winston Churchill, *The Second World War* (6 Vols., Boston: Houghton Mifflin, 1948–1953).
43. *The Private Papers of Senator Vandenberg*, p. 120.
44. If international law is drawn up by government lawyers to protect states' interests, "the result is almost sure to be an effort to preserve the *status quo*." Dulles, *War or Peace*, p. 199.
45. Sept. 17, 1947, *State Dept. Bulletin*, Sept. 28, 1947, p. 622.

46. Goodrich and Hambro wrote that inclusion of the phrase "encouraging the progressive development of international law" in Article 13 was due to "the insistence . . . that more emphasis be placed on law as a basis for the organization." *Charter of the United Nations*, p. 175.

47. *New York Times*, Sept. 16, 1955.

48. Corbett, *Law and Society*, p. 12.

49. *Ibid.*, pp. 288, 294, 295. This thesis was sharply disputed by Gerhart Niemeyer in "Relevant and Irrelevant Doctrines Concerning International Relations," *World Politics*, IV (1952).

50. Herbert W. Briggs, "New Dimensions in International Law," *American Political Science Review*, XLVI:698 (1952).

51. George Kennan, *American Diplomacy, 1900–1950* (Chicago: Univ. of Chicago, 1951), pp. 95–99.

52. That the official outlook has grown away from an earlier idea of law is illustrated by this recent statement by Ambassador Lodge, the U.S. Representative to the U.N.: "the huge world-wide influence which (the U.N.) exerts is a far more effective implement for peace than so-called 'legal powers' which, without the backing of public opinion, are but a dead letter." *New York Times Magazine*, Sept. 18, 1955, p. 14.

53. Kelsen, "Compulsory Arbitration of International Disputes," pp. 397–399.

54. See, among others, Kennan, *American Diplomacy*, and his more recent *Realities of American Foreign Policy* (Princeton, N. J.: Princeton, 1954); also Charles B. Marshall, *The Limits of Foreign Policy* (New York: Henry Holt, 1954); Harold Nicolson, *The Evolution of Diplomatic Method* (London: Constable, 1954); Hans Morgenthau, *In Defense of the National Interest* (New York: Knopf, 1951).

55. Administrative Tribunal *Judgments Nos. 18–38 (Doc.* AT/DEC/18–38) Aug. 21, 1953.

56. *Effect of Awards of Compensation Made by the United Nations Administrative Tribunal* (*I.C.J. Reports*, 1954), p. 47.

57. Ruggiero, *The History of European Liberalism*, p. 393.

Notes to Chapter 11 — *UNITED STATES FOREIGN POLICY*

1. In the "Truman Doctrine." Quoted in *A Decade of American Foreign Policy, Basic Documents 1941–9*, Senate Doc. 123, 81st Congress, 1st Sess. (Washington: Government Printing Office, 1950), p. 1256.

2. Gibbon, *The Decline and Fall of the Roman Empire*, ed. D. A. Saunders (New York: Viking, 1953), p. 35.

3. Walter Lippmann, *U.S. Foreign Policy* (Boston: Little, Brown, 1943), p. 53.

4. Secretary of State Dulles, quoted in *Department of State Bulletin*, Aug. 8, 1955, p. 221.
5. See Secretary Dulles' address to Foreign Policy Association, *Department of State Bulletin*, Feb. 28, 1955, p. 330.
6. *New York Times*, editorials, July 28 and Aug. 28, 1955.
7. As has been suggested by a number of writers, including Arnold Toynbee and Walter Lippmann.
8. Secretary Dulles, *Department of State Bulletin*, June 21, 1954, p. 937. See also Eisenhower-Churchill "Potomac Charter" statement, *New York Times*, June 30, 1954; Pacific Charter Sept. 8, 1954, and others.
9. Deputy Under Secretary Murphy, *Department of State Bulletin*, May 16, 1955, p. 801.
10. Machiavelli, *The Prince* (New York: Modern Library, 1950), p. 84.
11. Toynbee, *A Study of History*, p. 10.

Notes to Chapter 12 — *THE ERA OF PEACEFUL CHANGE*

1. Gibbon, *Decline and Fall*, p. 81.
2. Max Eastman, *Reflections on the Failure of Socialism* (New York: Devin-Adair, 1955), p. 105.
3. Hume, *Theory of Politics*, ed. F. Watkins (Austin: Univ. of Texas, 1953), pp. 84–85.
4. *Burke's Politics*, ed. Hoffman and Levack (New York: Knopf, 1949), p. 387.

Index